Religion: A Very Short Introduction

VERY SHORT INTRODUCTIONS are for anyone wanting a stimulating and accessible way into a new subject. They are written by experts, and have been translated into more than 45 different languages.

The series began in 1995, and now covers a wide variety of topics in every discipline. The VSI library currently contains over 650 volumes—a Very Short Introduction to everything from Psychology and Philosophy of Science to American History and Relativity—and continues to grow in every subject area.

Very Short Introductions available now:

Available soon:

For more information visit our web site

www.oup.com/vsi/

Thomas A. Tweed

RELIGION

A Very Short Introduction

OXFORD
UNIVERSITY PRESS

OXFORD
UNIVERSITY PRESS

Oxford University Press is a department of the University of Oxford.
It furthers the University's objective of excellence in research, scholarship,
and education by publishing worldwide. Oxford is a registered trade mark of
Oxford University Press in the UK and certain other countries.

Published in the United States of America by Oxford University Press
198 Madison Avenue, New York, NY 10016, United States of America.

Library of Congress Cataloging-in-Publication Data

Names: Tweed, Thomas A., author.
Title: Religion : a very short introduction / Thomas A. Tweed.
Description: New York : Oxford University Press, 2020. | Includes
bibliographical references and index. | Summary: "At a historical moment
when globalizing forces have intensified and two competing trends are at
work-religion is simultaneously bringing us people together and pulling
us people apart-everyone who aspires to be an informed global citizen
needs to understand religion. It doesn't matter whether you find
religion compelling or whether if your nation seems to be more and more
secular. What matters is that billions around the world practice a
faith-and that they act from it. It Religion shapes how they enter the
world and how they leave it, and how they eat, dress, marry-, and raise
their children. It shapes their assumptions about who they are and who
they want to be. Religion also identifies insiders and outsiders, who
has power and who does not. It both sanctifies injustice and combats it.
It draws national borders. It affects law, economy, and government. It
destroys and restores the environment. It starts wars and ends them.
Whether you notice it or not, religions play a role in how billions of
people conduct their lives. We are called, then, to understand this
important factor in human life today"- Provided by publisher.
Identifiers: LCCN 2020020752 | ISBN 9780190064679 (paperback) |
ISBN 9780190064693 (epub)
Subjects: LCSH: Religion.
Classification: LCC BL48 .T93 2020 | DDC 200—dc23
LC record available at https://lccn.loc.gov/2020020752

Printed by Integrated Books International, United States of America

For Bryn McNamee-Tweed and Kevin McNamee-Tweed, my beloved children

Contents

List of illustrations

Preface: Why religion matters

At a historical moment when globalizing forces have intensified and two competing trends are at work—religion is simultaneously bringing people together and pulling people apart—everyone who aspires to be an informed global citizen needs to understand religion. It doesn't matter whether you find religion compelling or if your nation seems to be more and more secular. What matters is that billions around the world practice a faith—and that they act from it. Religion shapes how they enter the world and how they leave it, and how they eat, dress, marry, and raise their children. It shapes their assumptions about who they are and who they want to be. Religion also identifies insiders and outsiders, who has power and who does not. It both sanctifies injustice and combats it. It draws national borders. It affects law, economy, and government. It destroys and restores the environment. It starts wars and ends them. Whether you notice it or not, religions play a role in how billions of people conduct their lives. We are called, then, to understand this important factor in human life today.

If you are not yet convinced that religion matters, I hope you will be by the end of this book. If you already see religion's significance, then what else do you need to know? That's the question I asked as I planned this book. You don't need to know everything, I decided, so my model shouldn't be Samuel Purchas's 1613 volume, whose subtitle promised a bit too much: *Relations of the World*

and the Religions Observed in All Ages and Places Discovered,
from the Creation unto this Present. I will, however, consider some
"ages and places," start the story earlier than expected, and bring
things "unto this Present."

You also need to know what religion is and how it has functioned
in human life. Since religion is not only about sacred books such
as the Bible and the Qur'ān, it is important to consider the
different ways religion is expressed, including how
communication and transportation technologies change how
religion is mediated. There is oxcart religion and jet plane
religion, printing press religion and computer religion. That's a
reminder that religion has changed over time. It has a history.
Some folks say it is the same in all times and places, or that there
is an underlying essence of true religion in all the world's great
traditions. There are indeed some continuities among the world's
religions, but it is important to know a little about how religion
emerged in the distant past and how it has changed through
history, including during the major lifeway transitions as humans
moved from foraging to farming to factories to fiber optics.

And, of course, we need to know something about religion today.
We need to know how it is easing and exacerbating global
problems and how the religious have engaged those of other faiths
in both horrific and uplifting ways. Finally, we must acknowledge
dystopian visions, gloomy predictions of how religion will prompt
us to blow each other up, and utopian visions, or more optimistic
accounts of how religion might be part of the solution to the
problems we face today.

Acknowledgments

A number of people and institutions helped, even though it is not their fault if errors remain. I wrote this while serving as director of the Rafat and Zoreen Ansari Institute for Global Engagement with Religion at the University of Notre Dame, and drafted chapters while a fellow at Notre Dame's Institute for Advanced Study. The Harold and Martha Welch endowed chair provided support. The College of Arts and Letters and the Keough School of Global Affairs gave me time off. Holly Googenbiller, Danae Jacobson, and Margaret Feigherty served as research assistants. My Notre Dame colleagues and those at many other universities have taught me a great deal. I could not have written this wide-ranging book without relying on the work of many scholars, even if I could not cite all that scholarship here. I also am grateful to the anonymous reviewers, and to my wonderful editor, Nancy Toff, and to Zara Cannon-Mohammed, Thomas Deva, and the rest of the staff at Oxford University Press. They all made the book better. So did Margaret McNamee, my dear wife, who remains my first reader. Finally, I dedicate this book to my children, Bryn McNamee-Tweed and Kevin McNamee-Tweed, life's great gift. They have always prompted more wonder than worry.

Chapter 1
What religion is

If religion matters, then definitions of it do too. Definitions have practical implications and real-life effects. Consider, for example, law and politics. Many political constitutions include the word *religion*. The First Amendment of the US Constitution states, "Congress shall make no law respecting an establishment of religion," and its second clause protects the "free exercise" of religion. Norway's 1814 constitution, the second oldest after the US document, also guarantees "free exercise," but it establishes a particular faith, the Evangelical Lutheran Church, as the state religion. In pluralistic Singapore, where four in ten residents are Buddhist, the constitution says that "every person has the right to profess and practise his religion and to propagate it." In spiritually diverse India, where Hinduism, Buddhism, Sikhism, and Jainism originated, the constitution guarantees "freedom of conscience and free profession, practice, and propagation of religion." The Canadian Charter of Rights and Freedoms also appeals to conscience while safeguarding the "freedom of conscience and religion." The Japanese constitution also guarantees freedom of "religion," and other political documents use similar language to protect freedom of "worship," as in Brazil, or the "practice of religion," as in Germany.

It is not always clear, however, what counts as religion, or what qualifies as religious practice. There are debates, sometimes passionate ones, about how to define it. I noticed the public implications of definitional squabbles when I served as an expert witness in a legal case in which I was asked to define religion for a US court. The case turned on a Florida defendant's use of African-inspired devotional practices that go back to West African techniques for curing illness, protecting people from harm, and divining the future. As the defendant was allegedly planning a crime, he visited a female conjurer—a ritual specialist—and placed cash in a Bible on the table between them and then asked for advice. During the 1930s, the folklorist Zora Neale Hurston observed a similar ritual practiced by an African American "herb doctor," as she called him, in rural South Carolina. I knew that and testified about the history of these practices, and suggested they could be understood, using a common definition, as religion. The prosecution—and, it turns out, the judge—did not think they qualified as religious, and so held that what the defendant said to the conjurer was not a confidential clerical communication.

I did not testify because I believed the defendant was innocent. I had no idea. I agreed because a constitutional principle was at stake, and I thought I might make a very small contribution to the public discourse about religion. I did not do much good, however, if the lawyers' comments during a break in my testimony were any indication. Before we returned to the courtroom, I overheard the attorneys for the prosecution reflecting on what I had said:

> "Can you believe this guy?" one blue suit asked the other in the hallway.

> "I know. That's *religion*?" his colleague asked incredulously.

Then they noticed me and tried to recover, since they soon would be asking me more questions on the witness stand.

> "Oh, well, very interesting, very interesting," the lead attorney said.

He didn't mean it. He thought any definition that included that ritual—and exonerated the defendant—was laughably, even tragically, wrong.

In this legal case, vernacular practices that share a great deal with long-standing Indigenous traditions in Africa, Asia, and the Americas were deemed secular because of unspoken assumptions. The attorneys and the judge seemed to presuppose that religion must have a formal institution and worship space, such as a church, synagogue, or mosque. Or maybe, ignoring the Bible on the conjurer's table, they assumed that the practice shared nothing with the "religions of the Book"—Judaism, Islam, and Christianity—or other traditions usually included in lists of major world religions, like those from China (Daoism and Confucianism) and India (Buddhism, Jainism, and Sikhism). Actually, such lists have changed over time and varied across cultures. Some interpreters since the nineteenth century, for example, have excluded Buddhism and Confucianism—because Buddhists do not believe in a personal creator and Confucians do not form church-like institutions. Such inclusions and exclusions have relied on more foundational assumptions about what religion is. So we need to think about that broader category and the consequences of definitions—and not only in courtrooms. Lawmakers sometimes need to borrow or create a working definition to make laws, and other professionals need one to interpret those guidelines, such as school officials, prison administrators, medical professionals, and those who must accommodate diverse spiritual practices.

The challenge of defining religion

One problem professionals face is that there are many definitions of religion—so many in fact that some scholars think we should not even try to define it. Thinkers in the modern West have offered contradictory views of what religion is, and since the rise of the academic study of religion in the late nineteenth century, the definitions have multiplied. In 1901 James Leuba, an American psychologist of religion, suggested we should stop trying, since no one could agree. The definitions have been, he suggested, "hopelessly contradictory" and "astonishingly diverse." To reinforce his point, he later published a list of more than four dozen definitions. That variety, Leuba suggested, showed that we cannot define religion—and should not try.

Others think we should not use the word *religion* because it is not a universal category: there is not an equivalent in every language. The term religion (*shūkyō*) only entered Japanese, for example, in the nineteenth century as Western influence rose. Some who point to this problem think we should substitute another word, like *culture* or *ritual*. One French scholar has suggested we take into account all comprehensive worldviews, religious and nonreligious, by talking about *cosmographic formations*. That would include the *Communist Manifesto* by Karl Marx and Friedrich Engels, as well the *Bhagavad Gītā*, a sacred text from India. Other critics complain that the term *religion* was coined in a colonial context, as Europeans subjugated peoples in Africa, Asia, and the Americas. For that reason, they suggest, it is morally tainted and descriptively slanted. And there is a final objection to definitions, especially those that emerged between the 1880s and the 1920s. Those definitions, critics point out, were linked with classification schemes that put the classifier's religion at the top of an evolutionary ladder and ranked the classified traditions below it. Those racialized schemes had terrible social consequences: they justified the maltreatment of Indigenous and non-Western peoples.

The critics have a point, but none of the objections mean we should give up on defining religion. The definitional variety shows that the word can be defined, not that it cannot. There are plenty of terms that constitute a field of study—like *art* and *literature*—that scholars disagree about. That does not mean they are disposable, and there certainly is disagreement about the alternative terms critics have proposed. As anthropologists know, for example, the word *culture* has been defined in countless ways. And while it is worth thinking more about a possible term for all comprehensive worldviews, *cosmographic formations* does not roll off the tongue. Further, using that category just shifts the debate to squabbles about what "comprehensive" means.

The other criticisms, grounded in moral observations about the colonial origin and social effects of the term, also do not require that we abandon efforts to define religion. Words that signal something like religion were used before the colonial period— before the British got to India, the Spanish anchored in the Americas, and the French landed in Africa. Yet it is true that colonial governors and Christian missionaries consolidated classificatory schemes that elevated themselves and demeaned others. As India specialists point out, the diverse beliefs and practices that came to be called *Hinduism* only became a single tradition when the British colonial administrators decided they had to count heads and control subjects. But we cannot toss the term. We are stuck with it. The word *religion* shapes political discourse and informs everyday speech. The disorienting variety, ambivalent history, and inequitable function of definitions only make our obligation to assess previous accounts and create better ones more challenging—and more morally urgent. Definitions matter.

Guiding metaphors and classic definitions

Definitions matter, in part, because they offer hints about theories, about what the definer thinks religion is. Definitions also tell us whether the author thinks religion is a good thing or a bad thing. Clues about these judgments can be found in the figurative language interpreters use. Nonliteral language, such as metaphor and simile, is not needed when English speakers point to an object they sit on and say "chair." That is the word they use. But some language is analogical, based on a direct or implied comparison between one thing and another. As in the Robert Burns poem, we might say "my Luve is like a red, red rose," using a simile, or perhaps convey our affection by saying "my Luve *is* a rose," using a metaphor. And interpreters have employed a wide array of analogies to describe religion. Consider a few of those guiding metaphors and similes as a way to glimpse the dizzying diversity of definitions—and introduce a few of the most helpful ones.

We can start with the definition given by Sigmund Freud, the Viennese founder of psychoanalysis. Many of his scientific beliefs have been discredited, though his therapeutic vocabulary still shapes contemporary speech, such as when we say a person is "repressed." Religion scholars also continue to ponder what Freud said, even if few accept all of his conclusions. Freud began his analysis of religion in 1907, with an intriguing but overlooked essay, "Obsessive Actions and Religious Practices." There he compared religious rituals to the compulsively repeated actions of those who, for example, must turn the door handle three times before they open it.

Freud's article offered a clue about what he would say in his 1927 volume *Future of an Illusion*. There Freud defined religion as "the universal obsessional neurosis of humanity; like the obsessional neurosis of children, it arose out of the Oedipus complex, out of the relation to the father." So his orienting metaphor was illness, and he drew on that analogy as he embedded several claims in his definition. First, Freud compares religion to a mental malady. Religion's origin is psychological and not social, cultural, political, or economic. Second, religion is a "universal" pathology, so it appears in all places and times. Third, since religion is "like the neurosis of children," followers are like children, and religion, like childhood, represents a lower stage of development. The implication, which Freud spelled out, is that religion will eventually be replaced by science—when humanity grows up.

Other unflattering definitions employ other orienting analogies and embed other foundational claims. For example, the nineteenth-century philosopher Karl Marx thought religion was a worldview that supported economic inequality by appeasing the masses, and, like a narcotic, keeps them drowsy. "It is," he argued, "the opium of the people."

Several theorists have used the analogy of a *system*, which emphasizes that a religion includes parts that form a whole. Using that metaphor too, Freud suggested that religion was "a system of willful illusions." Two other definitions also use this analogy. In 1912 the sociologist Émile Durkheim, who also introduced the distinction between sacred and profane realms, suggested that "a religion is a unified system of beliefs and practices relative to sacred things, that is to say, things set apart and forbidden— beliefs and practices which unite into one single moral community called a Church, all those who adhere to them." The anthropologist Clifford Geertz also appealed to the system metaphor in a 1966 essay. Religion, he suggested, is "(1) a cultural system of symbols which acts to (2) establish powerful, pervasive, and long-lasting moods and motivations in men by (3) formulating conceptions of a general order of existence and (4) clothing these conceptions with such an aura of factuality that (5) the moods and motivations seem uniquely realistic."

More recent characterizations also have used the metaphor of a system or, a related term, a *complex*. The sociologist Martin Riesebrodt suggested that religious practices are situated in a "web of meaning"—a metaphor Geertz used—but he also said religion is "a complex of practices that are based on the premise of the existence of superhuman powers, whether personal or impersonal, that are generally invisible." Another sociologist, Christian Smith, agrees but adds that the devout access superhuman powers "in hopes of realizing human goods and avoiding things bad." Another sociological definition uses system language while adding another concept (belonging) and a different analogy (a chain). Religion, for Danièle Hervieu-Léger, is "an ideological, practical, and symbolic system through which consciousness, both individual and collective, of belonging to a particular chain of belief is constituted, maintained, developed, and controlled." One advantage of the definition, she shows, is that it can provide language for describing how religion's "chain" of memory has been broken for many in secular western Europe.

Some theorists do not use system-talk but pick up on Durkheim's distinction between sacred and profane space, or "things set apart." They see religions as worlds of meaning that arise from encounters with "the Infinite" (Max Müller), "the Holy" (Rudolf Otto), or "the sacred" (Mircea Eliade). Each of these definitions relies on an understanding of humans' capacity for transformative experience. In a similar way, many interpreters have defined religion by emphasizing one or another psychic capacity—believing, feeling, or willing. In other words, there are intellectualist, affective, and volitional definitions. Religion is belief for many scholars, as in the anthropologist E. B. Tylor's 1871 definition: religion is "the belief in spiritual beings." But definers cannot agree about what adherents believe. Some say they believe in God, but others, like Durkheim, point to Buddhism's rejection of a personal creator god and try to broaden the concept.

Contemporary scholars influenced by neuroscience and cognitive psychology say religion is cognition; more specifically, they think about "counterintuitive supernatural agents," as the anthropologist Pascal Boyer proposed. Volitional definitions, which emphasize moral action or ritual action, have been less influential, but there have been a number of affective definitions that associate religion with feeling. For example, the theologian Friedrich Schleiermacher suggested that religion is the feeling of "absolute dependence." Some of the most hostile definitions have posited that religion originates in what the philosopher David Hume called "hopes and fears." Religion, Hume said, is "an anxious concern for happiness." In one of the most influential—and broadest—definitions, Paul Tillich said that religion is one's "ultimate concern," or whatever a person cares about most deeply.

That allowed him to include Nazism, which the German theologian had experienced before he fled to the United States in 1933. By extension, we might use that definition to say that Chinese Maoism, with its "Little Red Book" and veneration of Mao Zedong, was a religion too.

Some classic definitions combine several capacities, as Durkheim did by suggesting religion was about "beliefs *and* practices." The American psychologist and philosopher William James said in 1901 that he took religion to mean "the feelings, acts, and experiences of individual men in their solitude, so far as they apprehend themselves to stand in relation to whatever they may consider divine." That last phrase—"whatever they may consider divine"—made the category elastic, and the first phrase—about individuals and solitude—pointed to an important distinction. Some, like James, focus on the individual, while others, like Durkheim, see religion as arising from or equivalent to society. Religion is, he said, "an eminently collective thing." And many insist you cannot have religion without an institution, a social organization, as is the case with the anthropologist Melford Spiro's 1966 definition of religion "as an institution consisting of culturally patterned interaction with culturally postulated superhuman beings."

Religion has been defined in diverse ways. But how *should* we define it? Or, to ask a more useful question, what should an adequate definition do? My experience studying religion—and pondering its presence in public life—has led me to think that a good definition should do a few things. A definition should describe both content and function. In other words, it should say what religion is and what it does. Those interpretations that consider only content—like E. B. Tylor's "belief in spiritual beings"—fail to say how it affects individuals, shapes societies, and transforms environments. On the other hand, definitions that discuss only function cannot distinguish the religious from the nonreligious. To return to the functionalist definitions by Marx and Freud, it is difficult to decide whether a particular cultural practice is an "opiate" of the people or "a system of willful delusions." Could fiction function that way—leave us too dazed or deceived to see things as they are? How about television, film, sports, new media, or virtual reality? If so, how would we know what is distinctive about religion?

A definition must distinguish religion from nonreligion—as well as from related terms in popular discourse. Some observers of that courtroom scene, for example, might defend the conjurer consultation as *spirituality*, while some might ridicule it as *magic*. A useful description would help us decide whether it qualifies as religion, or whether another label might be better.

A definition should not settle the debate about religion's value in advance, before we start talking. It should not presume that religion is good or bad. We cannot describe it—as religion's debunkers do—only as psychological dysfunction or economic disempowerment. At the same time, we cannot define religion uncritically, as if it has been only positive. Further, those who think that only one religion is legitimate sometimes redefine the terms in an unhelpful way. They distinguish *religions*, understood as false human creations, from the one true *faith* revealed by God. The problem is that more than one group thinks it has the revealed truth, and that strategy, like the Freudian and Marxist approaches, closes off conversation before it begins.

A useful definition will attend to insider perspectives, which reflect how religion is experienced by adherents, and outsider perspectives, which reflect how religion is interpreted by nonadherents, including scholars. This is useful because specialists in the arts, humanities, and sciences can help us see how devotion relates to nonreligious processes, from neurons firing to nations fighting.

Finally, an effective definition is inclusive. It should neither minimize the complexity of religious life nor exclude the practices of some devotees. That means avoiding definitions that presuppose a single tradition (Christianity), one capacity (belief), a lone focus (the individual), one medium (texts), or a narrow segment of the global population (elite male Westerners).

To put it differently, we should avoid simplistic binaries that insist religion is either this or that. We need a *both/and* definition. An account that can interpret religion as it is practiced should acknowledge that devotion is about the individual and the community, body and mind, the home as well as the homeland. It should invite us to attend to women as well as men, the poor and the rich, those in the pews and in the pulpit, and those on the move as well as those who stay put. In a similar way, religion is about spatial orientation, as some definers say, but it also orients devotees in time. The religious use literal language to express their beliefs about the nature of things, but they also use nonliteral language like symbols, metaphors, and stories. The religious employ objects too, from prayer rugs to meditation cushions, and perform rituals, from baptisms to burials. Religion is transmitted by institutions (like Christian churches and Buddhist monasteries), as social scientists note, but it also is mediated by technologies (like jet planes and computers). And, yes, religion is about anxiety, including worrying about death. But to understand religion's complexity is to notice that it is about birth and natality as well as death and mortality. It's about the first cry of the infant and the last gasp of the dying. It's about seeking joy as well as confronting suffering. It's about wonder as well as worry.

Toward a definition

That shorthand—religion as worry and wonder—is not a bad place to start thinking about what religion is and how it functions. I have spent years tracing the global circulation of Buddhist texts, artifacts, and practices in the modern world, as well as studying

Cuban transnational migrants at a Miami Catholic shrine, where exiles use rituals, artifacts, and stories to move back and forth between the homeland and the new land. In both cases, religion is on the move. It is a process, not a thing. And religion-in-motion mixes with other traditions and with nonreligious forces. So when it came to offering a definition that made sense of the migrants' devotion but also might interpret practices in other times and places, I suggested that "religions are confluences of organic-cultural flows that intensify joy and confront suffering by drawing on human and suprahuman forces to make homes and cross boundaries." This dense definition needs some explaining, however. If I had said that in my courtroom testimony, the attorneys might have laughed even harder. Can't you just hear the one saying to the other, "It's about what? Confluences?" We could just stick with worry and wonder, I guess, but let me explain the guiding metaphors, identify the key commitments, and clarify the words and phrases.

This definition uses an uncommon term, *confluences*, which implies an aquatic metaphor, and a more familiar word, *crossing*, which alludes to a spatial analogy. Both make a similar point. Most definitions presume stasis and isolation, but religion, as it is practiced and as it unfolds, entails moving and mixing. Religion is a dynamic process and not an unchanging thing. It is not an object in a box.

To illustrate the *wrong* way to think about religion, consider the wooden cabinet I noticed in the Multi-Faith Prayer Room in London's Heathrow Airport. It had six cubes, each with a label showing that it was reserved for a different religious tradition: "Christian Faith," "Muslim Faith," "Buddhist Faith," and so on. Boston's Logan International Airport opened the world's first airport chapel in 1951, and these worship spaces are now commonplace. But that is not why it is important for our purposes. As with this cabinet and its cubes, some interpreters have imagined the world as containing a fixed number of static

1. The Multi-Faith Prayer Room at London's Heathrow Airport has a
cabinet in which each space is reserved for the ritual objects or sacred
books of a different religious tradition. The labels say, for example,
"Islamic Faith" and "Christian Faith."

and self-contained religions. Each tradition has its own space in
our mental cabinet, as is the case with those compartments for
Christian, Buddhist, and Muslim things. But this container
metaphor renders religions immobile and unchanging. To
understand global religions today, we need a different orienting
metaphor, one that allows us to attend to what happens as things
mix and people cross. So the first step in defining global religion is
to jettison the container model. That is why I use spatial images—
religion is about *crossing* and *dwelling*—as well as aquatic
metaphors—religions are "confluences of organic-cultural flows."

As odd as talk of "confluences" might be at first, it helps in two
ways. First, it offers a more resonant image for thinking about
what a religion is and how it changes. Some adherents think of a
religion as having a core that does not really change, as if it were a

13

mango with a leathery outer skin and inner pit covering a single seed. That misses something crucial about actual religious traditions: they are constantly changing and being changed. An aquatic metaphor is better because it puts religion in motion. It can help to think of religions as rivers or, better, "confluences of flows." So a particular religion, say Christianity, can be imagined as a surface where multiple streams converge to produce a wide river with tributaries entering and leaving. We might think of the early Christian communities, which spread the faith and produced the New Testament, as an aquifer feeding that riverine system in which, over the centuries, converging spiritual currents generated multiple ways of being Christian—Catholic, Protestant, and Orthodox. Each of those spiritual streams also has had intersecting creeks. There are hundreds, even thousands, of Protestant denominations, for example—like the Methodists and the Baptists. So the picture gets complicated. But, for me, that's good. Religion *is* complicated. I realize, though, that this aquatic metaphor might irk some who think their raft is the only vessel on the only stream. I am sorry about that, but, as I look out, I see lots of rafts and streams. Whatever its shortcomings as an analogy, talking about confluences captures the multiplicity of traditions and the dynamism of religion.

The talk of "confluences" helps in a second way. It provides terminology for thinking about how religions interact. It places interreligious exchange at the center of the picture. That helps, since all the religions I know have been formed in contact with other traditions and with the diverse forces that shape everyday life. That is why I say religions are "confluences of *organic-cultural* flows." Religion is both biological and cultural. It involves human bodies and natural ecologies as well as the cultural practices that dictate how devotees should adorn bodies and modify landscapes. In that sense this phrase meets one of the criteria for a useful definition—it invites outsider as well as insider perspectives by viewing religion in a way that welcomes insights from the natural and social sciences as well as the arts and humanities.

But there is still more to say to unpack this definition and note how it meets the other proposed criteria. This definition distinguishes religion from nonreligion, while still leaving room to talk about practices that have some but not all the features of religion. A practice, group, or artifact is religious if it appeals to "human and suprahuman forces," and, my fuller theory suggests, if it imagines a final crossing, "an ultimate horizon of human life," and a path to get there, whether the path is imagined as sudden or gradual and whether the end is understood as a place to go, like heaven, or a state of being, like enlightenment. By these standards, twelve-step recovery programs like Alcoholics Anonymous (AA) might count as religious, even if they say they are not, since they appeal to a supernatural force (a "higher power"), imagine a goal (sobriety), and propose a path (the twelve steps). But is that goal, sobriety, "an *ultimate* horizon"? I'm not sure. If you struggle with addiction, getting sober might seem most important. But I'm inclined to say that sobriety is probably not an ultimate aim. So maybe AA is *quasi-religious*, which means it has some but not all the features of religion.

Other labels also have to be ruled out. Some interpreters have dismissed practices as "superstition" or "magic." We need not take these terms too seriously, however, since they function mostly to denigrate. Opponents might classify consulting a conjurer as superstitious, even though they would insist that seeking counsel from a minister is religious. I don't see much difference. *Magic*, which means the manipulation of natural powers for personal ends, is also a divisive term. Historically, it has been employed by those who wanted to condemn Catholic ritual life, its "smells and bells," or the "strange" rituals of Indigenous Peoples in, say, Africa. In the history of the West, the term *magic* has been a weapon wielded in an interreligious battle. It is not a respectful label for sorting differences.

Another alternative, *spirituality*, deserves more serious attention. In an age when attending worship services has declined in western Europe and North America, the term *religion* has become more contested. A majority of adults in Portugal still describe themselves as religious, for example, but about half of those in the United Kingdom say they are neither religious nor spiritual. Most important for our purposes, about one in ten Europeans says they are "spiritual but not religious," and somewhat similar patterns hold in the United States and Australia. So what are these respondents saying? Most who identify as "spiritual but not religious" distrust religious institutions and their official creeds. But, curiously, they often say they believe in superhuman beings or powers, one feature of religion, and imply that they imagine an ultimate horizon of human life, another defining feature. So we could say their worldview is quasi-religious. Yet to honor their concern to distance themselves from all institutionalized traditions, it might be better to say that *spirituality* is not *religion*. However you label the institutionally unaffiliated (and those AA members), listing some defining features—the appeal to superhuman forces and the positing of an ultimate horizon—can advance the conversation about what counts as religion and what does not. Interpreters can at least give *reasons* for their judgment, one way or the other.

This inclusive definition, and the theory that extends it, also preserves religion's complexity. By acknowledging that the forces and beings devotees draw on are human or suprahuman, it accommodates Indigenous traditions that emphasize rituals to appease spirits, traditions like Buddhism that don't affirm a creator, and other traditions, like Daoism and Neo-Confucianism, that point to an indwelling principle (*chi*) or an impersonal force (*dao*). Think, for example, of *Star Wars*, which suggested "the Force" can be tapped into and used for good, as with Luke Skywalker, or for ill, as with Darth Vader.

The phrase "make homes and cross boundaries" also enlarges the religious realm. It includes those on the move: voluntary itinerants like travelers and forced migrants like slaves. At the same time, it leaves room to talk about the dynamism of religious practice, as in journeys to sacred sites. By focusing on "making homes," this account also allows us to include ordinary people, including women, who are marginalized by definitions that emphasize public institutions like the synagogue or the church, since men usually have had more power in those spaces. But almost everyone has a home, and (enlarging the scale) almost everyone has a homeland. So this account, which attends to both domestic spaces and communal boundaries, includes most devotees.

This definition is inclusive in other ways. Those who identify as religious might agree that they appeal to "suprahuman" beings or forces, even if they might not use that word. Many adherents also might say they turn to religion to "intensify joy and confront suffering." But does that phrase present too rosy a picture of how religion functions? Maybe. Many of religion's definers have minimized the search for joy and overlooked the experience of wonder. So let's keep that phrase about intensifying joy. But does "confront suffering" say all we want to say about how religion functions? It suggests that religion provides explanations for natural evil, like earthquakes, and techniques for dealing with moral evil, or suffering caused by humans. Zoroastrianism, the ancient religion of Iran and Central Asia, explains the source of evil: it teaches that there are two primordial entities, *Ahura Mazdā*, the benevolent force for order whom followers worship, and *Angra Mainyu*, the malevolent force for disorder whom they resist.

Positing a dualistic theology is one way of "confronting suffering." Yet, for some, this phrase in the definition still misses something important. When I have lectured in western Europe, young women and men who do not affiliate with a religion have questioned it. It is not that they don't think there is suffering. They see plenty. Their problem is that they think that religion has *caused* some of it. That, I think, is a very good point, and a helpful corrective. So let's say that clearly: whether it means leaders covering up sexual abuse, justifying racial injustice, or sanctioning gender inequality, sometimes religion *causes* the suffering devotees confront and the evil they must explain.

Chapter 2
What religion does

Some phrases in the definition I proposed specify how religion functions for the individual and for society. For example, as the devout "confront suffering" they find explanations for why things go wrong, and they "make homes" by using spiritual tools to transform the local ecology and construct symbolic worlds. But there is much more to say about what religion does. It also forms social bonds, creates collective identity, and provides spatial orientation. Religion gives private meaning but also wields public power. As adherents have appealed to religion's symbolic resources to assert power, they have both supported injustice and challenged it.

Cohesion, identity, and orientation

Religion creates social bonds. It's sticky. *Adherent*, the term for a follower, comes from a Latin verb (*adhaerēre*) that means "to stick together." So an adherent, the *Oxford English Dictionary* suggests, is a steadfast supporter who is bound by something, like a vow, or attached to something, like a cause. Spiritual attachments, I suggest, are of two kinds, and we can borrow terms from physics to distinguish them. Physicists use the word *cohesion* to refer to the force that holds like substances together; *adhesion* is the force that binds unlike substances. In a similar way, religion can be *cohesive*, creating in-group attachments among adherents, and, at its best, it also can be *adhesive*, creating bonds with those outside the group. Those bonds can be weaker or stronger, however, and problems can arise when a religious group is too sticky or not sticky enough. If a religious community lacks cohesion, it will lose members. But other problems—from isolation to aggression— arise when a religious community is too cohesive, when it is so tightly bound there is no space for adhesive forces to form ties with the wider culture and members of other communities. When inward-looking groups face outward with fear or fury, they can become, to coin a term, *dehisive*, a bond-breaking social force. The history of religion provides myriad examples of volatile religious movements that overemphasized in-group solidarity and escalated tensions with outsiders.

Religion also creates identity and provides orientation by situating the devotee in the body, the home, the homeland, and the cosmos. The religious set themselves apart by how they adorn their bodies. For instance, the Sikh followers of Gurū Nānak, the first of that Indian tradition's ten gurus, affirm guidelines imposed by the final guru. The identity-defining bodily practices that distinguished them from Hindus, Buddhists, and Jains are called the "Five Ks" because each begins with that letter in the Punjabi language: the devotee has uncut hair (*kesha*) and carries or wears a comb (*kangha*), steel bracelet (*kara*), sword (*kirpan*), and long underwear (*kaccha*).

Religion also situates devotees in the home and beyond the threshold of domestic space. It says you are from this family and this homeland, and that you have a special relationship with these gods, ancestors, or spirits. Religion maps social space and distinguishes *us* and *them*. It says the folks over the mountain have less powerful gods and less efficacious rituals. But even in one place, a religious worldview suggests, not everyone has the same status. Religion maps the social distance between community members. The ancient tradition of determining an individual's duty (*dharma*) according to stage in the life cycle and location in the caste system is detailed in Hindu texts like the *Laws of Manu* (*Mānavadharmaśāstra*), but that is only a well-known example of the social differentiation that happens in all religions. The process of identity-formation, of coming to understand your role in society and your place in the universe, starts early—Muslims whisper "God is Great" in the ears of newborns—and it continues through adulthood, as young Muslims learn that their most sacred site, the Kaʿba (or Kaaba), is in Mecca, where they face as they pray. In that sense, religion is watch and compass. It orients followers in time and space, mapping the near and the far and imagining an ancient past and an expected future.

Religion, in other words, is about moving across space and finding your place. Religious crossings can traverse water or land and can include foreign missions, holy wars, and pilgrimages as well as migration; but the religious also mark and cross stages in the life cycle and the threshold between this world and the next. The religious imagine something after death, a final crossing. Individuals and communities use what we can call *figurative tools*—analogical language like metaphors, symbolic actions like burials, and special buildings like temples—to transform the local ecology and construct an imagined world. In this sense, religion is homemaking. It is about making a dwelling place or, to borrow a term from the evolutionary biologists, constructing a niche. Humans' ecological-cultural niches are more complex than those of other animals—think of beaver dams—and religion's figurative tools have done some of that work of clearing the ground and making a world. Humans' cultural niches also can be transported. Migrants have carried niches and recreated new ones by combining the cultural materials they brought from afar with those they found nearby. In fact, much of global religious history has involved transoceanic and transcontinental migrants doing just that.

Yet niches also can be stressed, or even "cracked," to again use the biologists' language, and religion has both eased and exacerbated crises of sustainability. Problems have arisen not only when climatic conditions changed or residents depleted food sources. The term *sustainability*, as I am using it, has a broader meaning.

Most simply, a habitat is sustainable when the interplay between the community, the way of life, and the environment allows residents to meet "the needs of the present without compromising the ability of future generations to meet their own needs." And those "needs"—or conditions for flourishing—are cultural as well as ecological. For a habitat to be fully sustainable, I suggest, it must provide renewable resources, meaning and purpose, safety and health, equity and productivity, and as much individual freedom and political participation as the common good permits.

So culture—and religion in particular—plays a crucial role. How a local group or larger society deals with resources—and imagines economic, social, and political life—depends, in part, on how devotees use stories, artifacts, and rituals to understand themselves, their homeland, and their place in the wider universe. In turn, habitats can become stressed if one or two needs are not met, and unsustainable if multiple challenges converge—such as when resources diminish, disease devastates, injustice pervades, violence mounts, and religious worldviews no longer provide individual meaning and collective purpose. This broader notion of sustainability—and the talk of making and breaking niches—provides language for analyzing how the religious have experienced the big lifeway transitions, including the crisis moments when habitats have become less stable.

Meaning and power

Any account of what religion does must note that it also provides personal meaning and wields social power. Religions offer an account of the way the world is and the way it should be. They provide meaning by generating, in Geertz's language, "conceptions of a general order of existence." These conceptions are transmitted through story, reinforced in ritual, anchored in artifacts, and lived out in moral action. When the worldview is internalized by adherents, the "conception" provides a lens for seeing the world. These lenses provide glimpses of different worlds, sometimes very different worlds. That might be obvious if we think about the variety of views of, for example, the afterlife, but these worldviews also shape perception in less obvious and more mundane ways, including how a devotee might see a feature of the natural world such as a mountain or an ocean.

Many religions have something to say about oceans. They play a role, for example, in cosmogonic myths or creation stories. In some Indigenous myths from Polynesia and North America, land is assembled on the primordial ocean as a god, animal, or human dives down to bring up earth from the bottom of the sea. The ocean also makes an appearance in the first eleven chapters in Genesis—the first of two biblical creation stories: "in the beginning . . . the spirit of God was moving over the face of the waters." In a Hindu story a god created the waters and then laid his seed there. It became an egg, and from that primordial amniotic fluid the god Brahmā emerged. Similarly, the creation narrative in the *Popul Vuh*, which was composed by the Maya-K'iche' people of highland Guatemala in the sixteenth century and transcribed by a Catholic missionary in 1701–2, suggests that in the beginning was a void, with only the sky and the sea. Then gods from each realm went on to bring forth the world. Whatever adherents from these traditions might say as they gazed at an ocean, there would be differences—talk of one god and many gods, of earth-divers and cosmic eggs. These stories generate different worlds.

Oceanic metaphors were also employed by two influential religious thinkers from the thirteenth century who had very different worldviews: Dōgen, a Zen Buddhist monk in Japan, and Thomas Aquinas, a Dominican friar in Italy. They both turned to ocean analogies to describe what seemed difficult to express. In his *Summa theologiae*, Thomas suggested that God, "He Who Is," is not a being among other beings but "the infinite ocean of being." In that Christian world, the breaking waves become a chant of praise to the beauty of God's creation. Dōgen saw a different ocean. In his *Shōbōgenzō* (Treasury of the True Dharma Eye), he used the ocean metaphor to talk about the mind of the meditator and not the creator of the world. He seemed more inclined to cultivate detachment than express gratitude. He described an "oceanic" *samādhi*, a state of concentration in which the difference between the self and the other is transcended in an experience of oneness. Dōgen also referred to ocean waves in another text, noting that each drop of water splashing up from a crashing wave contains a reflection of the moon. The ocean, for him, prompted thoughts of impermanence—that everything is in flux, just as the meditator's distracted mind comes in and goes out like waves. And he thought of the Buddhist doctrine of interdependence—that everything is interconnected, though not as the effect of a First Cause, God, but as co-creator in a chain of causes. Aquinas thought that causal chain came to end at the "Unmoved Mover," and that the value of the ocean, and everything else, arises from its source, since "nothing is good and desirable except for as much as it participates in the likeness to God."

But what if a Christian wave watcher no longer believed in God's creative power, or a Buddhist beachgoer no longer found meaning in that interdependent world? Sometimes religion fails to serve its meaning-making function at moments of catastrophic disruption or cultural change. For example, many elite and middle-class Christian adherents were shaken by a Victorian spiritual crisis as intellectual challenges converged. Between 1840 and 1900 some lost faith in the face of Darwinian biology and the new geology, which challenged biblical claims about the origin and age of the universe; the new historical and literary study of the Bible, called Higher Criticism, which challenged the claim that scripture was divinely inspired; and the new comparative study of religions, which challenged the uniqueness and superiority of Christianity. Those doubters now looked out on a different ocean, as does the narrator in Matthew Arnold's poem "Dover Beach," who once found comfort as waves in "the sea of faith" drew near, but who now hears only "its melancholy, long, withdrawing roar."

Like Arnold's wave watcher, many Victorian doubters were sad, even tormented. And some struggled to retain their cradle faith by creatively reimaging traditional teachings. For example, that first creation story in the Book of Genesis says God made the world in seven days, but some theologians, thinkers who speak for the tradition, reinterpreted scripture more figuratively. It does not refer to seven twenty-four-hour periods but a series of evolutionary eras. Evolution, some Christians started to say around 1900, was God's way of doing things. In the twentieth century, religion's meaning-making function again came under fire, during the world wars, atom bombs, and the Holocaust, the Nazi-sponsored destruction of six million Jews in extermination camps during World War II. Some Jews, including the Auschwitz survivor Elie Wiesel, rebelled against the biblical God who was supposed to safeguard his chosen people. In his memoir *Night*, Wiesel recounted the protest that rose up in him as he watched children go to the camp's crematory, where their bodies were "turned into wreaths of smoke beneath a silent blue sky." Those moments, he said, "murdered my God and my soul."

But the Holocaust was a state-sponsored catastrophe in a predominantly Christian country, and Adolf Hitler's *Mein Kampf* had appealed to Christian themes to justify removal of the Jews. This reminds us that religion does not just provide personal meaning—or fail to do so. Religions, which claim ultimate authority, exert social power that can work for good or ill. Religion has functioned as a conserving force, defending unjust conditions, and as a transforming force, prompting social change. To illustrate, we could choose many examples, including the ways that the Church of England sanctioned slavery on the brutal sugar plantations in colonial Barbados and Protestant ministers in the United States defended slavery in the Cotton South during the nineteenth century. There are examples from Asia and Africa too, but the rise and fall of apartheid in South Africa offers an especially illuminating case study, since religion both supported the system of racial injustice and helped to bring it down.

A case study

In some ways the South Africa story starts in 1652 with the arrival of Dutch Calvinists, the first European settlers. Their descendants would be in power when the system of racial segregation called apartheid solidified, and when it crumbled during the second half of the twentieth century. But maybe a better place to start is 1893, when a London-trained Indian lawyer was kicked off a train for being a "coloured" in the first-class section. That lawyer, Mohandas K. Gandhi, had arrived to work among the South Asian merchants in Durban, and he faced a crossroads. As he remembered it in his autobiography, a question arose: "Should I fight for my rights or go back to India?" As you have already guessed, he stayed—and sent off a telegram to the head of the railroad the next day. Then Gandhi organized petitions, founded organizations, established newspapers, and, by 1906, launched his first "*satyāgraha* campaign." It was directed against an Asiatic Ordinance Bill requiring Asians in South Africa to register with the government so they could be grouped by color and culture.

Gandhi coined the term *satyāgraha*, which means "truth-force," to name the approach he initially had described as "passive resistance." He found better language in the work of Henry David Thoreau, an American who had been influenced by the US antislavery movement, as well as India's sacred texts. Gandhi was introduced to Thoreau's writings in London by a British reformer, and then, while working in South Africa in 1906, Gandhi read *Walden*, where Thoreau cited Hindu texts and said he sensed that "the pure Walden water is mingled with the sacred water of the Ganges."

Gandhi also appropriated ideas from the work of the Russian writer Leo Tolstoy, who had also read Thoreau. Tolstoy's *The Kingdom of God Is Within You* praised Christian pacifists and abolitionists and advocated "Christ's law of non-resistance." That meant refusing to participate in government-sponsored violence.

2. Images of an aging Mohandas Gandhi in traditional Indian dress are more familiar, but this photograph, taken when he was a lawyer in Johannesburg in 1906, shows his appearance when he was beginning his public activism in South Africa. On his left lapel Gandhi wears the badge of the London Vegetarian Society.

As much as Gandhi admired the Russian writer—and he named a South African community after him—he said later that "I took the name of my movement from Thoreau's essay" on "Resistance to Civil Government." That piece, which was retitled "Civil Disobedience" in later printings, also provided confirmation of the protest tactics Gandhi was trying in South Africa. Thoreau had penned that 1849 essay to explain his refusal to pay a tax: it was because the fees would fund the US government's immoral action to support African slavery, native displacement, and war with Mexico. And the citizen has a right, even a duty, to resist when conscience demands it, Thoreau argued. Gandhi agreed and employed peaceful forms of resistance, like marches, petitions, and boycotts.

Gandhi, who was raised as a Hindu but revered the Sermon on the Mount, might not have realized how much Thoreau's thinking had been influenced by Hindu texts. Thoreau had read in the *Laws of Manu* that nonviolence (*ahiṃsā*) is a central moral duty, and the New Englander praised the *Bhagavad Gītā*, which explored whether a warrior should kill others in war. Thoreau acknowledged those spiritual debts in a book he completed the same week he finished his essay on "Resistance." *A Week on the Concord and Merrimack Rivers* extended the principle of nonviolence to nonhumans. Thoreau asked about the effects of an upstream industrial dam on marine life: "Who hears the fishes when they cry?" Gandhi, a lifelong vegetarian, would have appreciated Thoreau's question. And the strategy for social change that Gandhi cooked up by combining a dash of different spiritual influences—and sifting them through his robust conscience— achieved a method of nonviolent resistance that helped win a partial lifting of the restrictions on Asians in 1914. The global flows continued after Gandhi turned his attention to the independence movement in his native India. For instance, even though a few critics say that during his campaign for the rights of Asians in South Africa he was "insufficiently anti-racist or anti-imperialist," African American church leaders reached out to

Gandhi between the 1920s and 1940s and later implemented nonviolent resistance in their mid-century civil rights movement, including during the Montgomery bus boycott.

Nonviolent resistance—and Christian social activism—also would play a role in the challenge to South African apartheid in the last decades of the twentieth century. The separation of the population along lines of color and culture was already in place in 1910, when the Union of South Africa formed, but the first explicit use of apartheid, a term meaning "apartness" in the Afrikaans language, was in 1948. The slogan "Keep South Africa White" helped the National Party win the whites-only election that year, and that white nationalist government, which was supported by Dutch Calvinist churches, passed a series of racist laws that segregated housing and education and banned interracial contact and marriage. It culminated in the forming of the Republic of South Africa in 1961, and the constitution of the new Christian state acknowledged "the sovereignty and guidance of Almighty God." Its preamble declared that God who "controls the destinies of nations and the history of peoples," had "gathered our forebears," and was guiding them to issue a "constitution best suited to the traditions and history of our land." In other words, God was on the side of the white Protestant minority. Religion was a conserving force that pulled people apart. It supported that inequitable policy.

In the decades ahead, however, black and white Christians denounced that official theology, and religion also became a transforming force that brought people together. The government used repressive tactics, imprisoning dissenters like the African National Congress leader Nelson Mandela and brutalizing protesters in the black township of Soweto in 1976, when hundreds died and thousands were arrested. The international community was slow to aid the black population, which was mostly Christian, but by the 1980s global and national church groups as well as the United Nations and multinational corporations implemented sanctions against South Africa. But there had been voices of protest in the churches and nonviolent resisters in the streets for decades. Some black ministers in the Dutch Reformed Church challenged the racial system, and so did Bishop Desmond Tutu, the Anglican advocate of nonviolent protest who was appointed leader of the South African Council of Churches in 1978 and awarded the Nobel Peace Prize in 1984.

The following year more than 150 unnamed theologians endorsed the "Kairos Document," a condemnation of apartheid. To protect those theologians, their names were not released, but we know that both black leaders, like the Reverend Frank Chikane, pastor of a pentecostal congregation emphasizing the power of the Holy Spirit, and white leaders, like Albert Nolan OP, a Catholic theologian who was a member of the same religious order as Aquinas, endorsed the long theological statement. The Kairos Document suggested God was issuing a "challenge to decisive action." It noted that there were Christians on both sides of the conflict, and identified three theologies being expressed. The "state theology" was misusing theological concepts and biblical texts as it "blesses injustice." The "church theology" was too passive, as it focused on "individual conversions" and failed to have the courage to effect real change. But the "prophetic theology," which the document endorsed, called for a liberation theology focused on decisive action, including civil disobedience: "A church that takes its responsibilities seriously in these circumstances will sometimes have to confront and to disobey the State in order to obey God."

Thanks to this impassioned theological criticism, as well as the use of the peaceful protest practices Gandhi had refined, South Africa's racist policies were abolished in the early 1990s. In 1993 Mandela, finally released from prison, and F. W. de Klerk, the South African president, jointly won the Nobel Peace Prize. The next year the country's black majority was able to vote for the first time, and Mandela was elected president. Two years later Tutu would chair the Truth and Reconciliation Commission, charged with investigating abuses under apartheid and seeking paths toward reconciliation. Locals say there is still much to do in South Africa, of course, but the changes between 1948 and 2004 offer hints about how religion can function both to preserve and oppose injustice.

The anti-apartheid movement communicated its message in varied ways. Everyday dissenters wore T-shirts with slogans, while elites released theological treatises. Gandhi had sent a telegram to protest his treatment on the train in 1893, but by the end of the struggle Bishop Tutu was doing interviews on television. That reminds us that we cannot just talk about what religion is and how it functions. It is also important to notice that religion is expressed in multiple ways. Religion engages all the senses, employs diverse cultural forms, and is mediated by varied technologies.

Chapter 3
How religion is expressed

Some adherents suggest religion is grounded in direct, unmediated experience. Spiritual writers who have spilled a lot of ink telling us they had an ecstatic experience they cannot describe have turned to oceanic metaphors—as with Dōgen—to recall their feeling of becoming one with everything, as a drop merges into an ocean. Or, like Teresa of Ávila, they use the analogy of sexual intimacy to suggest those experiences were encounters with a beloved. Her description came to life in Gian Lorenzo Bernini's sculpture of Teresa's "ecstasy" as her heart is pierced by a flaming spear that left her "completely afire with great love for God." Her head thrown back, that sixteenth-century Spanish mystic seems to be in a moment of erotic rapture.

These Christian and Buddhist writers describe transformative experiences, but ecstatic experiences are always mediated by bodies and cultures. They are generated by sensory impressions and framed by learned language, for example. So, on the one hand, religion begins and ends with bodies. The impulse to worry and wonder arises in a body where neural circuits transmit messages and the limbic system directs sensory input. Yet devotees also use cultural practices and communication technologies endorsed by the social institutions that formed them. And if we overlook these mediating processes and expressive modes, we can't understand how religion takes hold: how it can

3. Gian Lorenzo Bernini's statue called *The Ecstasy of St. Teresa* (1647–52) is in a chapel within Santa Maria della Vittoria, a church in Rome, Italy. The artist portrays Teresa's moment of "ecstasy," her passionate encounter with God.

inspire the imagination, prod the conscience, and stir the emotions. So let's think first about bodies and the senses, and then consider cultures and the eight modes of religious expression.

Bodies

To say that bodies mediate religion is not to split mind and body or to isolate nature from culture. Religions are *confluences* of organic-cultural flows. Things converge. But bodies do not get their due, so let's start there.

Bodies constrain but do not determine religious experience. It matters that humans have two eyes facing forward and a cerebral cortex with billions of neurons for higher-order thinking. Consider, for example, how embodied processes affect thinking and feeling.

The brain shapes cognition, including thinking about time and space. Most important, it regulates religion's function as watch and compass. Cultural practices inform spatial orientation, but it always begins with biologically constrained bodies. The perception of space emerges from embodied persons interacting with sensorial environments encountered through sound, smell, taste, touch, and sight. And there are two kinds of spatial cognition. They are associated with distinct regions of the brain and, in turn, correspond to two forms of mapping: *autocentric* (self-centered) and *allocentric* (object-oriented). Autocentric thinking involves the parietal neocortex, draws on cognitive processes involved in action and attention, and orients humans in the immediate environment. Space is framed in terms of the embodied subject— the head-feet axis, the front-back axis, and the left-right axis. A kneeling devotee at a shrine, for example, might say that the image of the saint is *above*. In contrast, allocentric or object-centered cognition involves the hippocampus and adjacent cortical structures and concerns great distances and long-term spatial memory. It helps humans navigate space beyond the body.

That space is represented in terms of fixed, not relative, points—for example, north and south or, in religious worlds, Jerusalem and Mecca. And there can be no religion without the imagining of distant spaces, not only sacred centers but also the ultimate horizon of human life, however that is understood.

Spatial navigation and memory processes are linked. The hippocampus, the seahorse-shaped area beneath the cortex, plays a role in both spatial sensing and episodic memory. Long-term memories are indexed by the location of the event, whether the devotee was walking in a religious procession or kneeling at home to pray. Even if the landmarks are taken away, such as when migrants leave familiar sacred spaces, the mental and emotional associations remain. The feel for the event's space and time isn't lost when the site is distant. So we need to notice hippocampal neurons firing to understand, for example, the hold of the homeland and the persistence of the past. Religion is irrevocably *transtemporal*, propelling devotees back and forth in time, as well as *translocative*, moving them back and forth in space. We might lose sight of this unless we attend to embodied processes involved in temporal and spatial cognition.

But religion is about feeling too, and emotion is shaped by how brains work as well as how cultures signify. Interpreters debate whether emotions are universal, occurring everywhere, or culturally specific. One intriguing argument for the commonalty of emotional responses comes from Mengzi, or Master Meng, who lived in late Zhou dynasty China (1040–221 BCE), when leaders justified their rule by claiming it was mandated by Heaven (*tiān*), which they understood as something between a personal god and an impersonal force. We know what this early Confucian philosopher taught, because his disciples gathered his sayings and dialogues into a collection we call the *Mengzi*, or *Mencius*, which was edited in the second century of the common era (CE). Mengzi wanted to refute contemporaries who said either that humans are naturally self-interested or that there is no fixed human nature and a person's environment makes them who they are. By contrast, Mengzi believed all people are born with four ethical dispositions or moral tendencies (benevolence, righteousness, wisdom, and propriety), and each is associated with a corresponding feeling. We can detect those implanted moral "sprouts," which grow if cultivated, by observing emotional reactions. For example, Mengzi argued, the feeling of compassion arises from the inborn virtue of benevolence (*rén*). As evidence, he invited his disciples to conduct a thought experiment: "Suppose someone suddenly saw a child about to fall into a well." He believed that "anyone in such a situation would have a feeling of alarm and compassion," so people are basically good and compassion is a universal sentiment.

Using different arguments, some interpreters have claimed there is a universal religious emotion. Rudolf Otto, for example, called it *mysterium tremendum*. When a person encounters the holy, he proposed, she feels a combination of awe, wonder, fascination, and fear. Otto resorted to marine analogies: "The feeling of it may at times come sweeping like a gentle tide, pervading the mind with a tranquil mood of deepest worship." That brings us back to oceans, and some interpreters nominated "oceanic feeling" as a defining religious emotion. Freud used the phrase in a 1930 book, but he appropriated it from a letter he received from a Nobel Prize-winning French writer, Romain Rolland, who got the idea from a Hindu teacher, Ramakrishna. In that letter, Rolland encouraged Freud to consider "spontaneous religious sentiment . . . the simple and direct fact of the feeling of the 'eternal' . . . ," which he described as "oceanic," limitless like the ocean.

Freud agreed, but he decided it was a bad thing, a regression to an earlier developmental stage when infants have a feeling of unity with the world. Infants cannot tell where their body ends and the world begins. But oceanic feeling is not, as Rolland thought, the source of religion. Rather, Freud suggested, religion springs from an infantile feeling of helplessness, which prompts humans to imagine a divine father who will make everything better. Rolland, who lost his Catholic faith but found Hindu thought, was not defending the divine Father he had revered as a boy. He was advocating a more primal experience described by the Bengali-born mystic Ramakrishna, who adapted a long-standing Indian religious tradition to claim that in the highest state of concentration an "individual soul loses its limited existence when it falls into the ocean of Brahman," or ultimate reality.

We can find approximations of that feeling expressed in multiple traditions, as seen in the ecstatic visions of the twelfth-century Sufi mystic Rūzbihān Baqlī, who said he was related to God "as a drop is to the ocean." Yet religiously inflected emotions are always rooted in a particular time and place. They can be quite specific. Ghanaian pentecostal migrants in Chicago, for example, worry about being perceived as outsiders because they are black and foreign, and these newcomers turn to local congregations to find the shared sentiment they most need—social trust. Rather than search for a single religious emotion, then, it might be more helpful to emphasize that, even if some feelings might be transcultural, almost any sentiment can be symbolically and ritually coded as religious.

Consider worry and wonder, which I have emphasized, and the related emotions of sadness and joy. There are many reasons to cry, but tears can be experienced as religious when they arise in a ritual setting and symbolic community. The spontaneous shedding of tears is the parasympathetic nervous system's response to physical pain or intense affect, and the pious have reported that tears can fall because of the blissful presence of the holy, as Teresa said, or the anguished absence of the holy, which St. John of the Cross called the soul's "dark night." There also can be tears of joy at wedding rituals and tears of sorrow at funeral services. In those mourning rites, weeping can be scripted or spontaneous. In the West, only spontaneous tears seem to count, but among Yoruban devotees in Nigeria, for example, the public performance of mourning can be a meaningful collective ritual. In any case, grief can be a religiously inflected emotion. So can wonder. That mix of curiosity and elation arises when a person encounters the unexpected, something that does not fit the labels we usually apply. It is experienced, some scientists think, when neurons are activated in both the limbic system and the "association cortex," which integrates sensory information. There are also communal forms of a related emotion that Émile Durkheim called "collective effervescence," a shared feeling that arises during intense communal rituals. Mediated by neural networks, religions offer ways of experiencing and expressing varied feelings, including those understood as most negative and most positive.

The senses

To complete this sketch of how bodies mediate religion we need to say more about that sensory input. Religion is about the senses, first, because it prescribes practices to control them. A collection of ancient South Asian texts, known as the Upanishads (*Upaniṣads*), suggested that you cannot reach the religious goal unless you control the senses, as a charioteer might snap the reins to control his horses. Augustine of Hippo, a fifth-century North African, turned to a different image to make a similar point in his *Confessions*. This bishop, who gave in to sexual desire before he became a Christian, suggested that he had become enslaved by the "chain of habit" forged when he succumbed to impulses channeled by the senses. To break that "chain," Augustine argued, the Christian must turn from the carnal to the spiritual. In the more extreme form of control, there is *asceticism*, practices that affect bodily needs and redirect sensual signals. There have been pole-sitting Christian ascetics who battled the senses in the Sahara Desert and wandering Hindu ascetics who did the same on the rainy Indian subcontinent. But controlling the senses also might mean, for example, taking a vow of celibacy, as Catholic nuns do, or fasting during the month of Ramaḍān, as Muslims do.

And the senses matter in another way: as it is lived in daily life, religion engages all the senses. Followers create "sensory cultures" that affect thinking, prompt action, and provoke emotion. The sacred music of Johann Sebastian Bach, for example, can elicit a range of emotions—from tearful gratitude to awe-struck joy. This eighteenth-century composer, who believed that "music was instituted by the Spirit of God," worked at St. Thomas Church, a Lutheran congregation in Leipzig, Germany. There he led the choir and orchestra that performed during worship services, including at special moments in the liturgical calendar, like Easter and Christmas. At the first performance of Bach's *St. Matthew Passion* on Good Friday in 1727, the violin's mournful minor chords and the soprano's high-pitched lament reminded the undeserving sinner of Christ's redemptive suffering. Several years later, on Christmas day, the first part of his *Christmas Oratorio* lifted up the penitents gathered at the church, as the choir, trumpets, flutes, and strings built to a rousing celebration of Jesus's birth that might have enraptured even the most hard-hearted congregant. In different ways, East Asian Buddhists have included music in their celebrations of Buddha's birthday, and Sunni Muslims have their own sonic practices associated with the birth of the Prophet Muhammad (570–632 CE). The *mīlād*, a gathering during the month of his birth, involves a sequence of sound events that begin and end with prayer but include hymns (*naʿt*) chanted in unison by the worship community.

The sonic expression of religion takes even more forms. The most ancient expressions of music, or "humanly ordered sound," employed drums, flutes, and voices at gatherings led by a shaman, a ritual specialist who healed the community, buried the dead, and foretold the future. With the development of writing systems, devotees recited or chanted sacred texts, and sound also announced the beginning or end of rituals. The *shofar*, or ram's horn, is blown on the Jewish holy day Rosh Hashanah, the New Year, and at the conclusion of Yom Kippur, the most solemn day of the year. Church bells announce the start of Sunday service, and the Muslim call to prayer (adhān) is heard five times each day, from before dawn until after dusk. There are slight variations in the Shiʿi and Sunni adhāns, though in both major Islamic traditions it begins with the muezzin chanting Allāhu Akbar (God is most great) four times and ends with lā ʾilāha illa llāh, the emotionally evocative phrase testifying that there is "no God but God."

Smell, taste, and touch can be as important as sound. As for the olfactory, consider the ritual use of incense, the burning of substances like sandalwood, camphor, or cedar to produce an aroma. The Magi, or Wise Men, brought the infant Jesus frankincense and myrrh, which were used for burnt offerings, though before the late fourth century many church leaders condemned the practice because Christians' refusal to offer incense to the Roman emperor and the "pagan" gods had defined Jesus's early followers. Yet "a lavishly olfactory piety" became part of Christianity by the fifth century, and burning incense has been used in that and other traditions for purification, healing, and to send wishes aloft to God or the gods. It even has been used for timekeeping: in Japanese Buddhist temples the presiding monk watched the stick of incense burn to tell when it was time to stop meditating and begin the next communal activity.

Incense burning remains part of everyday life in some places, including Taipei, Taiwan. Researchers found that about four in ten households on that East Asian island burn incense twice a day, and it wafts across Taipei's cityscape, where pedestrians can smell it rising from hidden alleyway altars and prominent downtown temples. The wider metropolitan area has more than one thousand temples, including Longshan, which is Buddhist, and Baoan, which is Daoist. There is so much perfumed piety that scientists have studied the negative effects on, for example, air pollution and heart disease, and in response leaders at those two temples have decreased the number of incense pots and restricted the number of sticks devotees can place in each one. That is their

4. Chinese Malaysian devotees offer incense sticks at a temple in the city of Melaka during a New Year's celebration in 2018.

way of trying to reduce the environmental and health effects, though other evidence suggests incense also can have a positive impact on mood. That is because, unlike the other senses, smell directly engages the region of the temporal lobes where memories are stored and emotions are triggered. As a devotee who grew up smelling incense at a Daoist temple in Taipei, or at a Catholic church in Rome, might confirm, the scent of incense can trigger deep emotional reactions.

Ingesting things is religious practice too. Every year a group of the Huichol (or Wixárika) from Mexico go on a three-hundred-mile pilgrimage to Wirikúta, the high-desert homeland where they eat bitter-tasting divine peyote, a psychoactive substance that induces visions that, the pilgrims hope, might restore their health and sense of purpose. Some traditions prohibit foods, as seen in the rules against pork for Muslims, against meat for Hindus, and against pork and shellfish for Jews. Religions also tell you what you should eat, drink, or inhale. Inhaling the fumes of burned plants like tobacco was an important ritual among Indigenous woodland communities in North America, and for hundreds of years the chief of Mississippian communities passed around a purifying "black drink" made from a holly leaf that induces vomiting. At archaeological sites around the world, excavators have uncovered evidence of feasting, of ritual banquets after the hunt (for foragers) or the harvest (for farmers). The religious also celebrate smaller-scale meals, as with the Jewish Passover Seder, which commemorates the Israelites' escape from bondage, and the Christian communion meal, which commemorates Jesus's Last Supper.

In many traditions, the gods need food too, and to bridge the gap between the sacred and the profane, followers even ingest material associated with a holy figure. As in most African Indigenous traditions on the continent and in the diaspora, adherents honor the supreme being who is the source of life, but they also appeal to lesser gods, as is the case with Afro-Cuban devotees who place offerings on altars that include tastes that the òrìṣà prefers: Ọ̀ṣun, a goddess who helps with fertility, is fond of sweet things like honey or oranges. Similar ritual logic applies when Hindu, Daoist, or Buddhist devotees place food offerings on home shrines or temple altars in Asia. Medieval Christians and Muslims even ingested relics, bits of the bodies or possessions of revered figures. And in the Catholic view of communion, the priest's words and gestures transform the wheat host into the "real presence" of the body of Christ. Even though theologians offer a loftier interpretation, that ritual is about tasting the divine.

The devout also touch things with their fingers, feet, and lips. On the night before his crucifixion, around 30 CE, Jesus humbled himself to wash the feet of his disciples, and on Holy Thursday Christians across the world gather to repeat that tactile ritual. Performing another ritual that goes back to the late fourth century, Christian pilgrims to Jerusalem try to walk where Jesus walked and touch what he touched. Some gather pebbles or scoop up dirt to take home. Jews living in Israel can visit the Western Wall of the destroyed Second Temple and place written prayers in its crevices, just as Japanese devotees at the main Shintō shrine in Ise City write their request for the Sun Goddess and other spirits (*kami*) on a small wooden plaque they hang at the site. Devotees in India reach out to touch the Hindu deity being carried through their village during a festival procession, and Russian Orthodox Christians go farther: they kiss icons, painted images of Jesus and Mary, a tactile piety that slowly and lovingly wears away those devotional images. Touch is also a metaphor for contact with the transcendent—as in "touched by the spirit"—and it is highlighted in Michelangelo's painting *Creation of Adam* on the ceiling of Rome's Sistine Chapel. The artist, who finished that scene in 1511, created a mood of expectation by placing the almost-touching fingers of Adam and God at the center. It would not have been nearly as powerful if he had portrayed the next moment, when the divine had already given life to the first human. The suspense heightens the viewer's appreciation for the power of touch.

But devotees are also forbidden to touch some things. For example, in the second-century rabbinic code of rules called the Mishnah, Jews are told to avoid touching the Torah scroll, their sacred text. But that rule presents a practical problem, since rabbis chant Torah passages in the synagogue and need to keep their place. In a creative adaptation, at least since the seventeenth century rabbis have used a Torah pointer, or "hand" (*yad*), a thin ceremonial object that often includes an index finger at the tip, where it touches the untouchable text.

Finally, religion also involves seeing. But, as with the other senses, religious elites sometimes restrict what can be seen and who can see it. Only the high priest of the ancient Temple of Jerusalem could see the holy of holies, the most sacred chamber, and only on Yom Kippur, the Day of Atonement. And even if there has been a

5. This Jewish ritual object, a Torah pointer, was made in Austria in 1862 and used by rabbis to keep their place in the sacred text.

rich material culture associated with Jewish religious life— including Torah pointers—the Hebrew Bible condemns making images. In other words, Jews have been aniconic, suspicious of visual representations of the divine. Even writing the name of God risks idolatry. Observant Jews omit some letters in the word G-d to honor their conviction that the divine is beyond representations. Muslims share that belief. Just as Abraham destroyed images of competing gods, Muhammad rejected the polytheism that thrived around Mecca in his day and insisted Muslims avoid depicting God. But Islamic artisans can use Arabic calligraphic script from the Qurʾān, as well as geometric and botanical designs, to decorate artifacts and architecture, as with the Qurʾānic inscriptions on the interior walls of the Dome of the Rock (692 CE) in Jerusalem.

Other traditions, like Sikhism, also have been aniconic. Its founder, Gurū Nānak, rejected the visual splendor of the Hindu temples around him, and suggested that the divine "cannot be fashioned, it cannot be made." Some Christians turned away from the icon-loving materiality of the Catholic and Orthodox faiths. Early Protestants associated with the sixteenth-century movement that came to be called the Reformation began by stripping altars of images. Aniconic impulses also have survived into the twenty-first century. The Taliban, a Sunni group that interprets Islamic law strictly and governed most of Afghanistan from 1996 to 2001, issued an edict against religious images. Then, in 2001, they blew up two enormous 1,500-year-old Buddhas at Bāmiyān, a cave-temple complex northwest of Kabul, Afghanistan.

Despite worries about idolatry, images have been important in multiple traditions. For Hindus, worship includes *darśan* (pronounced dar-shan), which means seeing and being seen by a deity at a temple, and followers of other traditions have venerated many gods. To glimpse the astonishing variety of supernatural beings imaged in material form you might tour a museum near you, or search a museum's online collection for keywords like "religion" "god," or "goddess." At the British Museum, for example, you can find images from Hindu, Buddhist, Jain, and Christian traditions, as well as everything from a bronze Egyptian cat representing the goddess Bastet made about 30 BCE to a fifteenth-century Aztec eagle from Central America carved in volcanic rock and associated with the solar god Tonatiuh.

The modes of expression

So the body plays a role as a conduit of religion, but religion also is expressed culturally, from the music of Bach to the philosophy of Mengzi. It can help to distinguish these diverse cultural expressions—even if they are usually interconnected. There are eight overlapping modes of cultural expression, I suggest, and for each we can identify a characteristic action and a cultural domain. *Experiencing* refers to embodied engagement with the environment, but religion is also about *imagining*, *narrating*, *making*, *conceptualizing*, *enacting*, *performing*, and *gathering*.

The eight modes of religious expression

Action	Domain	Example
Experiencing	Embodied and perceptual	Rūzbihān's oceanic mysticism or Teresa's ecstatic encounter
Imagining	Symbolic and analogical	Muhammad as the "seal" of the prophets or the symbol of the cross
Making	Material and architectural	A torah pointer or a Shintō shrine
Narrating	Mythic and literary	A creation story in the Mayan *Popul Vuh* or the Hindu *Rigveda*
Conceptualizing	Doctrinal and philosophical	*The Mengzi* or *Summa theologiae*
Enacting	Ethical and legal	The Ten Commandments or the five Buddhist precepts
Performing	Ceremonial and performative	Burning incense at a Daoist temple or performing Bach's *Christmas Oratorio*
Gathering	Social and institutional	The Roman Catholic Church or Shingon Buddhist Sect (*Shingon-shū*)

Imagining and narrating

Religious *imagining* refers to the use of tropes or nonliteral language to represent the seen and the unseen. There are many figures of speech, including symbol, metaphor, simile, allegory, and narrative. Many scholars of religion have emphasized symbols—words, images, or gestures that point beyond the simple one-to-one correspondence of a sign. So, a Stop sign on the road is not a symbol. It has only one meaning: bring your vehicle to a stop here. But there is no single meaning of, say, a Christian cross, Buddhist wheel, or Jewish star—or the primary Jain symbol, an ancient swastika surrounded by three dots and a half moon. The half-moon at the top represents the abode of liberated souls, the three dots are the paths to liberation, and the four arms of the swastika refer to the four cosmic realms. However, because Adolf Hitler misappropriated the swastika as an emblem for Nazi Germany, it has become troubling, especially in the West. On the 2,500th anniversary of Mahavira's final liberation in 1974, India's Jains released a new official symbol, which adds an image representing *ahiṃsā*, or nonviolence, but retains the swastika that adorns many ancient Indian statues and temples. Because of the negative connotations, however, North American Jains replaced the swastika with the sacred Sanskrit syllable *om*. As this example shows, symbols can evoke powerful feelings and change over time. But symbolic thinking is important, scholars suggest, since it inclines humans to seek hidden meanings and allows them to tell stories that explain the world.

There is more to say about narrative, but analogical language, speech that compares one thing to another, is even more fundamental. The analogical imagination relies on the ability to cross different areas of knowledge and associate unlike things. Christians, for example, say Jesus is the Lamb (*amnos*) of God (John 1:29) and thereby move between how we think about animals and how we think about humans, imagining Jesus as a sacrificial offering. Buddhists draw on medical analogies to interpret the Buddha as the Great Physician (*bhisakka*) who diagnoses and cures humans' spiritual maladies. Muslims declare that Muhammad is the Seal (*khātam*) of the prophets (Qur'ān 33:40), and thereby move between how we think about documents and how we think about humans, imagining Muhammad as a waxy sealant that closes and authenticates a prophetic lineage. Religion requires not only neural compasses and biological clocks, but also the capacity to speak and act as if something—for example, a lamb, or anything else in the mundane world's literal referents—can be something else too. A lamb sometimes can be just a lamb, but analogical artifacts, ritual performance, and shared stories can also cross cognitive domains. The devout can suggest that a man was sacrificially slaughtered "like a lamb." Followers can say that a man without medical training provided the cure they sought. The pious can suggest that a man was a sealant on a document. This sort of imagining is one way that religion is expressed.

It is also expressed by telling stories. *Narrating* engages multiple senses—hearing as well as seeing—and can take many cultural forms, like painted scenes and staged drama as well as oral tales and written texts. Humans have been telling stories for thousands of years, and oral storytelling has remained important among Indigenous Peoples from Australian Aboriginals to Scandinavian Sámi. Stories also have found their way into holy books, texts that a community deems authoritative. Some traditions authorize more than one. Jews, for instance, consult both the Hebrew scriptures and rabbinic writings. Muslims value both their holy book, the Qurʾān, and the Sunna, the example of the Prophet, who serves as a model of exemplary behavior. That is why the sayings and deeds of Muhammad, known as Ḥadīth (Arabic for "report" or "news"), constitute a secondary scripture that is exceeded in authority only by the Qurʾān. Buddhists have more than one book too. They have multiple collections of sūtras, or sacred texts, in different languages that are known as the Pali, Sanskrit, Tibetan, and Chinese canons.

Those holy books tell stories using diverse literary forms, including poetry or hymns. For example, one of the 1,028 hymns in India's oldest sacred text, the *Rigveda*, recounts how Indra separated heaven and earth by killing the demon Vritra. As in this Hindu work composed between 1400 and 1000 BCE, religious narratives also present a cast of animal, human, and superhuman characters; describe earthly, subterranean, and celestial settings; and unfold a plot in historical or mythic time. And stories build on other stories. Indra, the warrior god of the Vedas, makes an appearance in later Hindu texts like the *Bhagavad Gītā*, which was inserted into the larger *Mahābhārata* between the second century BCE and the second century CE. The authors assume the devotee already knows Indra—and all the characters, settings, and plots of the Vedic hymns. Similar intertextual gesturing happens in the holy books of Jews (Hebrew scripture), Christians (New Testament), and Muslims (Qurʾān). They all have a place for Abraham in their stories, for instance, but add characters, shift settings, and alter plots as sacred stories are told, disputed, and retold. Muslim commentators have interpreted a passage in the Qurʾān about Abraham building "the House" (2:125–128) as referring to the cube-shaped Kaʿba in Mecca, for example—a story that Jews and Christians reject in favor of the account in Genesis (13:18) suggesting that he built an altar in Hebron, a West Bank town.

The narratives inscribed in holy books are not only read. They are recited, heard, memorized, chanted, pictured, and performed. The term *Qurʾān*, which was given to the revelations that Muhammad conveyed starting in 610 CE, is related to the Arabic word for "recite." It evokes orality more than literacy, and captures the aural aspect of Islamic practice. Muslim children memorize verses from the Arabic text, and then learn to recite entire Sūras, or chapters. Accomplished adult Qurʾānic reciters become famous in the Islamic world, and recordings of their verbal performances circulate in multiple media. Some textual narratives are also performed, as with the *Mahābhārata*, the long Hindu epic. Drumming and dancing accompany the staged retelling in Indian Himalayan villages, and Indonesian Hindus put on shadow puppet performances of this epic. Holy books can also become works of visual art, as with the Book of Kells. That illuminated Latin manuscript of the Gospels was created around 800 CE in a monastery off Scotland's western coast, and it includes, for example, an intricately ornamented page introducing Matthew's story of Jesus's birth. Other sacred books designed for ritual purposes also function as visual expressions of piety. Consider medieval Jewish, Christian, and Muslim holy books that have decorative "carpet pages"—called that because they look like Persian rugs—including the gold-framed page preceding the Book of Exodus in a tenth-century Torah with Arabic script that was produced by and for Jews living in Islamic Palestine or Egypt.

Narrative and ornament are juxtaposed in other artifacts, like the twelfth-century altar cross from Britain called the Cloisters Cross, a twelve-inch ivory symbol with ninety-two images and ninety-eight inscriptions, including a depiction of Jesus as Lamb of God and a story of Jesus's resurrection. Story and image mix in less elaborate objects too, such as the tin *ex voto* paintings created by village artisans in nineteenth-century Mexico that fulfilled a promise or expressed gratitude to a saint. Ordinary Catholics often commissioned these devotional objects to document a miracle—and then hung them at home or donated them to a church. In one *ex voto* made in 1825, for example, the anonymous artisan who memorialized the miracle painted vivid red flames rising from the devotee's kitchen. The Spanish writing below the painting tells the viewer that the resident, Silberio Agilar, had promised he would commission the painting if Christ, who is depicted at the top, prevented the rest of his house from going up in flames. Christ came through—and so did Silberio.

Making

Narrating can inspire *making*, crafting artifacts and transforming spaces, but the material expression of religion includes more than devotional paintings and illuminated books. There are mundane things like clothing: the orange robes of a Thai Buddhist monk, the white tunic of a Zoroastrian magus in India, and the black head covering of a Saudi woman. There are ritual objects, like the altar cross, Torah pointer, and incense pot. In West Africa, priests use divination trays to discern an individual's future. Hand-held prayer beads are used to keep track of prayers or recitations in Islam, Catholicism, Hinduism, Sikhism, and Buddhism. There is also architecture, like the sixty-four square miles of Angkor Wat, the twelfth-century sandstone temple complex in Cambodia dedicated to the Hindu god Vishnu; the spiral minaret (or tower) and blue mosaics of the ninth-century Great Mosque of Sāmarā in Iraq; and the soaring verticality of Chartres, the thirteenth-century Gothic cathedral dedicated to Mary, supported by flying buttresses, and illumined by 167 stained glass windows.

There has been an enormous variety of spaces set apart for solitary, familial, or communal devotion. These can be as small as a shelf in a home, but also include larger communal spaces designed for different spiritual purposes: to house the gods or the people, or to enclose human remains or the relics of holy figures, as with Buddhist stupas and Christian shrines. Ritual spaces' interior design can direct the visitors' attention to the spoken word or the performed ritual, as with the difference between a pulpit-centered Protestant church and an altar-focused Catholic church. The labels for worship spaces offer other clues about differences as well as continuities. A *gurdwara*, the term for a Sikh worship space, means "gateway," and it signals that devotees pass through the gate that leads to the guru. *Agyari*, a place of fire, is the term for a Parsi temple that preserves the Zoroastrians' sacred flame. The term mosque (*masjid* in Arabic) refers to a "place of prostration," where worshippers prostrate themselves before God. Members of the Bahá'í faith worship at a *Mashriqu'l-Adhkár*, in Arabic, "a place where the mention of God rises at dawn," or a "dawning place of the praise of God." It refers to a gathering of followers reciting scripture to praise God, especially at the morning's first light. *Cathedral* is a term that Anglicans and Catholics use for a special church where the bishop's seat, or *cathedra*, can be found, highlighting not only institutional leaders (bishops) but also ecclesiastical regions (dioceses). *Synagogue*, the term for a Jewish worship center, comes from a Greek verb meaning "to gather together," so it is a site where a community assembles.

These architectural labels signal that *performing*, or ritual action, and *gathering*, or communal congregating, happen there. Some of these buildings also have been sites for *conceptualizing* the tradition's beliefs. Chartres Cathedral, for example, sponsored a school, and the building's design and ornamentation reflected theological perspectives that cherished light, proportion, and clarity—including the clear expression of doctrines in the stone sculpture and polychromatic windows. At a time when few were literate, Chartres was a visual catechism, a material expression of doctrinal commitments.

Conceptualizing

The academic study of religion has mischaracterized lived religion by making too much of doctrine, but we need to give *conceptualizing* its due. Most adult adherents can say something about what they believe, and, if their tradition has creeds, many can repeat official doctrinal statements. But creating and revising doctrinal systems requires learning and leisure. Conceptualizing is an elite enterprise. It often has been the work of male religious professionals living apart from the community, or remaining within it but freed from other social responsibilities, so they can study and write.

There are impressive examples of doctrinal treatises from many traditions. Three prominent thinkers from the twelfth and thirteenth centuries incorporated Aristotle's philosophical categories in works addressed to Muslim, Jewish, and Christian communities. Ibn Rushd, known in the West as Averroës, was born in Cordoba, Spain, in 1126. This scholar of Islamic law also was the first to construct a systematic Islamic philosophy based on the writings of Aristotle. Born nine years after Ibn Rushd, in the same city, the Jewish thinker Moses Maimonides also came to deeply engage Aristotle's philosophy, though he strove to balance reason and revelation more than the rationalist Ibn Rushd. Maimonides fled to Egypt, where he wrote—in Arabic, not Hebrew—his influential philosophical work, *The Guide of the Perplexed*. In that text, he suggested that Jews needed no surer foundation for belief than the Bible, but for intellectuals who sought answers for themselves or their Muslim and Christian neighbors, Maimonides provided a rational system that presented Judaism's beliefs as true and its moral principles as rational. He suggested that Jews could reconcile revelation in the Bible, which uses analogical language, and insights from philosophy, which employs literal language.

The Christian Aristotelian who tried to reconcile reason and revelation was Thomas Aquinas, the Italian thinker we met earlier. His *Summa theologiae* (Summation of Theology), which he was still writing when he died in 1274, dealt with God, creation, and humanity in the first part. It addressed morality and law next, and the unfinished third part dealt with more narrowly Christian doctrines about the incarnation of Jesus and the sacraments of the church. Even if the *Summa* did not win universal acclaim, its basic strategy came to have extraordinary influence. Thomas argued that philosophical reason can prove that God exists, but reason eventually needs revelation, the unveiling of God in history, to understand what is true and good.

These reason-loving writers illustrate this mode of cultural expression, but some thinkers who engaged concepts aimed to show the unreliability of reason. Some Western mystics did that, and so did some classic Chinese texts in the Daoist and Buddhist traditions. The eighth-century Buddhist text *The Platform Sūtra of the Sixth Patriarch* emphasized the sudden mind-to-mind transmission of insight, which is beyond words and inaccessible to reason. The author, the Chan Buddhist master Huìnéng, taught that humans have "inherent enlightenment," even if it is not always evident. Just as the sun is always bright but cannot always be seen, "the floating clouds of false thoughts" can cover the individual's Buddha-nature. Only proper meditative practice, not conceptual schemes, can clear the clouds and let the light through. The *Zhuangzi*, a Daoist text compiled around 300 CE, also disparaged reason and demeaned concepts. This work, which purports to represent the teachings of Zhuangzi, suggests that one cannot find the Way (*dao*) by rational reflection. The text shows the limits of conceptual analysis by frustrating the reader in passages like this: "Making a point to show that a point is not a point is not as good as making a nonpoint to show that a point is not a point." If you don't know what that means, join the club. That, I think, is the point. Sometimes Zhuangzi also makes the point that is no point—or, at least, not a reasoned conclusion—by relaying perplexing stories, like this one: "One night, Zhuangzi dreamed of being a butterfly—a happy butterfly, showing off and doing as he pleased, unaware of being Zhuangzi. Suddenly he awoke, drowsily, Zhuangzi again. And he could not tell whether it was Zhaungzi who had dreamt the butterfly or the butterfly dreaming Zhuangzi. But there must be some difference between them!" That poke at rationality is found in a text created by elites engaged with ideas, but it does not function like the texts of those Aristotelian rationalists. It invites the reader to rethink what is true and real, while also gesturing to a nonrational path. Just as the *Platform Sūtra* advocated "no-thought" (*wunien*) and proposed a path for discovering the individual's inherent wisdom, the *Zhuangzi* advocated "non-action" (*wuwei*) and proposed a path that relies on the person's inborn capacity to act spontaneously in accord with the *dao*, the originating source and ideal pattern of all things.

Enacting and performing

In both its rationalist and anti-rationalist forms, conceptualizing has been less central for most traditions than morality and ritual, even if many faiths say that right belief is part of the spiritual path. Often the conceptual is entangled with the ethical and the performative. The *Bhagavad Gītā*, for example, identifies three Hindu paths: the path of knowledge (*jñanamarga*), devotion (*bhaktimarga*), and action (*karmamarga*). Many sayings attributed to the Buddha present him as more pragmatic than rationalist. He tells followers to ignore philosophical questions and focus on the matter at hand—ending suffering. Yet the

"Eightfold Path" described in the classic *Turning of the Wheel of Dharma (Dharmacakrapravartana-sūtra)* suggests the Buddha taught that proper understanding was required for achieving the goal of *nirvāṇa*, the blissful release from suffering. That eightfold path to liberation basically amounted to achieving wisdom (right view and right intention), being moral (right speech, right action, right livelihood), and enhancing concentration (right effort, right mindfulness, and right concentration).

The intellectual, the ethical, and the performative also intermingle in the Muslim summary of obligations, the Five Pillars of Islam: the witness (*shahāda*), the prayer (*ṣalāt*), almsgiving (*zakāt*), fasting (*ṣawm*), and pilgrimage (*ḥajj*). The first entails professing foundational beliefs—that there is no God but Allah and that Muhammad is His Messenger. The other four involve ritual practices—performing daily prayers, fasting during the ninth month (Ramaḍān), and going on pilgrimage to Mecca if you are financially and physically able. It might seem that the remaining pillar, *zakāt*, is about ethics, since it concerns giving to the less fortunate, but Muslims also see this as an act of worship, as it is done to express thanks for what you have.

Christians have no universally accepted roadmap for the spiritual path, but many would point to this exchange with Jesus in the Gospel of Matthew (22:34–40): "'Teacher, which is the great commandment in the law?' And he said to him, 'You shall love the Lord your God with all your heart, and with all your soul, and with all your mind. This is the great and first commandment. And a second is like it, You shall love your neighbor as yourself. On these two commandments depend all the law and the prophets.'" Some might add the moral and ritual guidelines announced in the Sermon on the Mount (Matthew 5–7), which includes the Lord's Prayer and Jesus's advice on prayer, fasting, and almsgiving—don't do them hypocritically or boastfully—as well as other principles and practices that chart a path through "the narrow gate" of Christianity. Don't just avoid killing, you should not even allow

6. Muslim pilgrims try to touch the doors of the Holy Ka'ba in Mecca during the final phase of the annual pilgrimage to Islam's holiest city.

anger to rise; and when they strike you, turn the other cheek. Don't just love your neighbor, but love her or him as yourself and go farther: love your enemies too.

As this overview hints, most spiritual paths detail guidelines for moral action, principles or rules to enact. In other words, traditions have something to say about morality, religiously sanctioned and culturally transmitted norms governing how humans interact with one another, with other animals, and with the wider environment. These moral rules concern the individual—providing a model of a worthwhile life and offering guidance for daily decisions. Traditions also transmit rules about the social order (who can marry) and the political order (who can use force). These guidelines might be unwritten codes or written rules like the Ten Commandments or the lay Buddhist's five precepts, which prohibit killing, stealing, lying, abusing intoxicants, and sexual misconduct. For a socially marginalized group, its moral tradition might concentrate on governance of the religious community and how members should interact with those with political power. For religiously sanctioned empires that achieve regional dominance, such as the pre-Columbian Inca in Peru or post-Constantinian Christians in Europe, leaders rely on local custom and spiritual principles to develop a system of governance that details the tribute owed to the capital and the rights granted to the provinces. In medieval societies where Muslims formed the majority, a complex legal system called *sharīʿa* developed. Since less than one-tenth of the 6,346 verses in the Qurʾān have the form of a law—and many concern ritual duties—Muslims looked also to the example of the prophet as revealed in the Ḥadīth and relied on the consensus of legal scholars and the rulings of judges to determine the rights and obligations of both Muslims and non-Muslims.

Whether their tradition's moral and legal rules were commanded by a god or discovered by a person, communities often have codified such guidelines in interaction with other faiths. Jainism emerged out of Hinduism in India in the sixth century BCE, and followers accepted that tradition's conceptual scheme, including the view that karma drives the cycles of existence and that liberation (*mokṣa*) from those cycles (the ultimate aim) can be achieved by seeking wisdom and bodily control. Yet Jains also became known for their distinctive emphasis on *ahiṃsā*, or noninjury, which they expanded to include every form of life. In a similar way, Jews and Christians both embraced the Ten Commandments, or the Decalogue. This list indicated what you should *not* do. In Matthew's Gospel, Jesus added prescriptions (what you should do) to the proscriptions (what you shouldn't), and the Sermon on the Mount expanded the requirements of Jewish law to include, for example, love of one's enemies, and warned that the Christian's obligation involves more than just doing the right thing. You also have to do it in the right way and for the right reason. These guidelines did not emerge in isolation, however. The Gospel of Matthew was written about 80 CE, ten years after the fall of the temple in Jerusalem, and it was intended for Greek-speaking Jewish and Gentile Christians in Syria who were negotiating their new relationship to the Jewish community and the Torah's teachings. Jesus's Sermon on the Mount accepts a great deal in Jewish law and doctrine, even if the Matthean community also was proclaiming that the messiah had come and God's Kingdom was near, views that neither the Jews who preceded them nor the Muslims who followed would affirm. Islam offered a somewhat parallel decalogue in the Qurʾān (17:22–40) but did not mention Jesus's sermon. However, a parallel Qurʾānic passage (2:271) advocates not bragging about almsgiving, and an eleventh-century Islamic philosopher, Abū Ḥāmid al-Ghazzālī, praised Jesus's suggestion to turn the other cheek.

Traditions also established guidelines for performing religious rituals, which are collectively formalized, invariantly performed, and institutionally transmitted actions and utterances that refer to supernatural forces and ultimate matters. That means spoken words—"I now pronounce you husband and wife"—can be ritual, a speech-act, just as hand gestures and bodily movements can. It also means that rituals presuppose a social setting, a group, not just an individual. You cannot sit alone in your room and invent a religious ritual. Well, you could, but it would not qualify as ritual unless you convinced others to perform it too. And they would have to do it the same way each time. That is what "invariant" means. Ritual requires repetition. Innovation is possible. That has happened in the history of religion, but the community—or a subgroup—must agree about the change and then teach it to the next generation. To decide if an action qualifies as religious ritual, ask if you could imagine someone saying this after observing it: "No, that's not how we do it!" If so, then it is a ritual, since the response implies that there is a proper way to perform the action, and the use of "we" suggests the practice was collectively created and passed down in a community. If an action has those features but does not concern gods, saints, or ancestors, and does not reflect a worldview that posits an ultimate aim for human life—then it might be ritual, but it is not *religious* ritual.

Formalized, invariant, and transmitted practices have taken many forms. Ritualized action might be as simple as a Catholic school girl making the sign of the cross in Manilla's Binondo Church—quickly touching her right hand to her forehead, chest, and shoulders—or as complicated as a white-clad Japanese widower making the walking pilgrimage to the eighty-eight temples of Shikoku, traveling with Shingon Buddhism's ninth-century founder Kūkai, who, pilgrims say, always walks beside you. These rituals are done alone, but ceremonies also can be performed in a group. And they can take place at sites designated as sacred, or in everyday spaces like a passenger train or a living room. There can be high- and low-emotion rituals. And rites also can serve different purposes, even if most involve contact between the human and the supernatural. In spirit possession rituals, a masked dancer temporarily *becomes* that spirit; other rituals chase off annoying spirits that are bringing harm. Rituals can happen once a day, week, season, or year—or only once in a lifetime. Calendrical rituals, for example, happen during a season, such as the rainmaking ritual of the Chewa of Mozambique, who pray to their Supreme Being, Chiuta, and make shrine offerings at the end of the rainy season.

Life-cycle rituals mark the transition in status that occurs when an individual is born, named, matures, marries, ages, or dies. These rites of passage usually involve three stages: *separation*, in which the person moves outside of the social order and its identity markers; *liminalty*, in which the ritual subject is between, or on the "threshold" between one status and another; and *reintegration*, when the person reenters the community with a new identity—as a wife, in a marriage ceremony, or as an ancestor, in a burial rite. To illustrate, consider initiation rituals among the Mande and other peoples who live in Sierra Leone, Liberia, Guinea, and Côte d'Ivoire. During puberty the boys and girls are separated, and elders take them to live in a specially constructed village in the forest for a year. There they learn the secrets of the Poro (male) and Sande (female) initiatory societies, and then undergo ritual scarification and circumcision to mark their changed status. They arrive as children, and, at the end of the year, return as adults.

Gathering

Such coming-of-age rites require a social group that transmits the guidelines for how to act. In the same way, the other seven modes of expression also depend on *gathering*, with adherents coming together. The sociologist Max Weber distinguished religious and political organizations and classified forms of spiritual organizations and types of religious leaders. A "hierocratic" organization, or *church*, is a sacred group whose members are born into it and whose leaders exert psychological control over a territory by distributing or withholding religious benefits. A "political" organization, or *state*, is a secular group whose members are born into it and whose leaders safeguard order in a territory by the threat or use of physical force. In some early hunting and gathering bands, which feature shaman as ritual specialists, the political and the religious realms merge, and membership in both is hereditary. That merging also happened in larger agricultural societies organized into chiefdoms or kingdoms, which featured a *priest* or *priestess* performing rituals at a stationary place of worship, like the priestess who presided at the central Greek temple dedicated to Athena. And Weber suggested that a *prophet* also might appear, a figure who proclaims a revelation as a mouthpiece of a god (like Muhammad) or who discovers the message proclaimed (like the Buddha).

Weber also distinguished the large inclusive *church*, with its authorized priests, formalized routines, and hereditary members, from the small exclusive *sect*, a voluntary group that admits only persons with specific religious qualifications. In other words, sectarian membership is not automatic or based on heredity. You have to convert or pass a religious test to be a member. Other scholars of religion and society have added subtypes of churches and sects, as well as other organizational categories, like *denomination*, an established division within a larger church, and *cult*, a small group organized around a "charismatic" leader, one whose authority comes from the leader's personal appeal and not his or her institutional role. The terms *church* and *denomination* are useful for describing the social expression of Christianity. But since the word *cult* has lost its intended meaning and become a derogatory term, it is best to avoid it, even for controversial Christian-inspired movements like the People's Temple, whose 900 members died in a mass murder-suicide in Guyana in 1978. We can instead refer to those groups as *new religious movements* (NRMs), a broader category with fewer negative associations.

The *church/sect/denomination* classification is of some comparative use: for example, Japanese Buddhism has institutional forms that look a lot like Protestant denominations. But such classification can distort our understanding of non-Christian communal modes of expression. For cross-cultural comparison, it is better to talk about *religions*, *sects*, and *new religious movements*. The *religions* can be classified on a continuum by size (from large to small), scope (from global to local), and membership (by birth or by choice). There are large and inclusive global religions, like Christianity and Islam, that welcome both converts and those born into the faith. Some more localized and exclusive Indigenous traditions are identified with a particular people and a particular homeland. The plural term *religions* refers to broad traditions that have the most adherents today—Christianity, Islam, Hinduism, and Buddhism—as well as those that claim fewer practitioners, such as Judaism, Sikhism, Zoroastrianism, Confucianism, and Jainism.

These broad labels can obscure the diversity *within* religions, however. Divisions arise and new sects form. You might think of such sects as tributaries of a river. Or, if you prefer arboreal images, branches from a tree. And those branches have had influence. *The Platform Sūtra of the Sixth Patriarch* was a

How religion is expressed

polemical text that contrasted the "sudden" approach of the patriarch, Master Huìnéng, with the "gradual" approach of his Chan Buddhist opponent. When that sudden form of Chan, the "meditation" sect, migrated to Japan, it emerged as a distinct religious institution, Sōtō-shū, that competed with other Buddhist sects, including the Shingon-shū that pilgrims celebrate at Shikoku. The differences between Protestant and Catholic worship spaces also reflect institutional splits that began in the sixteenth century. Those who "protested" continued to quarrel among themselves, and those differences were institutionalized in many Protestant sects or denominations.

The variations in the Muslim call to prayer reflect differences between the Sunni majority and Shiʿi minority, two major branches of Islam. They have disagreed about Islamic law and, especially, about who should lead the Muslim community after the death of Muhammad. During the first centuries of Islam, the majority of Muslims accepted the *khalīfa* or caliph (successor) of Muhammad as the authoritative religious and political leaders, but those who came to be called Shiʿi believed that authoritative leadership was found in a hereditary lineage that descended from the fourth caliph, Ali, Muhammad's cousin and son-in-law, who was assassinated in 661. That Shiʿi minority viewed Ali's descendants as their spiritual leaders, or Imams.

Finally, there are also new religious movements (NRMs). Christianity and Islam were once new movements. They succeeded. So did Baháʾí and Mormonism, both of which arose in the nineteenth century and have a global presence today. Baháʾí emerged from Iranian Islam. Its prophet, Baháʾuʾlláh, announced in 1863 that he was the manifestation of God for that era. The Baháʾí faith affirms the oneness of God and the centrality of justice, but it diverges from Islam in its doctrine of progressive revelation, the belief that each age requires a new manifestation of God. That faith also designated a different spiritual center—not Mecca, but two shrines in present-day Israel. The Latter-day

Saints (LDS), or Mormons, emerged from within American Christianity. Their founder, Joseph Smith, translated new revelations given to him on ancient brass plates by an angel, and his early followers published them as *The Book of Mormon* in 1830. By 1847 Mormon migrants had founded Salt Lake City as the spiritual center of the group, which came to be the Church of Jesus Christ of Latter-day Saints.

Conclusion

Religions, sects, and NRMs have created distinct institutions, like the LDS Church, but religious practice has been mediated by the technologies that the devout employ as well as the institutions they organize. We can see the mediating power of technologies and institutions—and note institutional splits—by reconsidering the Bāmiyān cave-temple complex, where yellow-robed Buddhist monks once gathered in a monastery and used ancient communication technology to write Sanskrit texts on palm leaves.

In that valley along the Silk Road route to China, India, and Persia, and beneath the two cliff-dwelling Buddhas, a thousand monks lived out their faith amid the aroma of incense and the sound of chanting. In the monasteries below, early sectarian divisions were evident. The Bāmiyān monks aligned themselves with the Lokottaravādin school, which arose during Buddhism's first schism. That early debate concerned the proper religious ideal. It focused on whether the *arhat*, a person who has achieved enlightenment, is perfect. The monastic order at Bāmiyān descended from those who challenged the *arhat* ideal affirmed by the other original Buddhist schools, which their opponents would call the Hīnayāna, or "Lesser Vehicle." They decided that those who achieve liberation are fallible. That opened a slight gap between humans and buddhas, and it led to the development of the Mahāyāna, those who called themselves the "Greater Vehicle." That major Buddhist branch, which dominated East Asia, proposed an alternative ideal: the wise and compassionate

7. An 1834 engraving of the Buddhas in Bāmiyān, Afghanistan, shows how the statues looked before they were destroyed. The people and camels at the base of the larger Buddha, which was about 175 feet tall, give some sense of their monumental size.

bodhisattva, who renounces his own liberation to save all beings. They also venerated buddhas as supernatural agents with wondrous powers, a view already expressed in the Mahāyāna texts stored in the library at Bāmiyān and hinted at in the cave temple's sculpture and murals, including those colossal Buddhas. So those Bāmiyān monks, who gathered in monasteries and wrote on palm leaves, were the inheritors of one institutional split and forerunners of another.

The later history of that cave-temple complex reminds us that mediating institutions and technologies can change. The Bāmiyān monastic community that built those Buddhas in the sixth century CE continued after Islam entered the region. Yet the Mongol ruler Genghis Khan damaged the temple complex in 1222, and late-Mughal emperors (1526–1857) even used the standing Buddhas for target practice. Changes continued after the Taliban, who communicated with silicon chips instead of palm leaves, dynamited the enormous statues in 2001. Supporters were unable to rebuild the colossal images, so those hoping to recover the Afghan Buddhist past resorted to new technologies. In 2015 a Chinese couple donated a device to project 3-D images of the standing Buddhas onto their original alcoves, and for a few moments in the early evening of June 6 they were virtually restored to the cliffs.

Chapter 4
How religion has changed

Because the past shapes the present, responsible citizenship also requires some sense of history, an idea that applies particularly to the matter of religion. Too often public discussions of the religious dimensions of policy issues either overlook the past or concentrate on very recent years. But that shortened perspective makes it difficult to see what is new and what is not—and which problems, such as climate change, economic disparity, and interreligious violence, are entangled in a longer past. We need a history that traces religion's role in the broad changes in ways of life, from foraging to farming to factories.

The emergence of foraging religion

We cannot pinpoint when religion began, since there are no written sources to tell us what we want to know. But we can recall religion's defining features and expressive modes and identify the cognitive, social, and ecological conditions necessary for religion to emerge. Then we can ask when we can see those conditions in the material evidence dug up by archaeologists.

Religious action is always mediated by technology and institutions, constrained by human biology and the local ecology, and lived out with creatively appropriated cultural resources— figurative language, ceremonial artifacts, moral codes, and ritual practices. But all these factors require certain biological capacities, environmental conditions, and social forms. The fragmentary material evidence—the stones and bones—does not allow us to settle the scholarly debate about whether those conditions arose abruptly or gradually. But the appearance of a few capacities was crucial. Ritual performance, material creativity, and moral action depend on empathy (the ability to detect what others feel) and imitation (the ability to do what others do). They also require gathering, forms of social organization, and the religious must cooperate closely and communicate skillfully in extrafamilial groups, so they can circulate moral guidelines, shared beliefs, and ritual practices.

The appeal to superhuman forces and the imagining of ultimate aims requires certain cognitive processes. To ask and answer the big questions—like where did I come from and what will happen when I die?—the devout must be able to imagine beginnings and endings, the origin of things and the end of things. A ritual burial, for instance, makes no sense unless the mourners have some idea of an afterlife, and that forward-looking perspective requires the capacity for complex spatial and temporal representation. That means religion was possible only when our ancestors' brains had evolved enough to do such things.

Finally, the religious employ tropes, or nonliteral language, to express all that. So they needed *figurative tools* for making and remaking imagined worlds; in other words, they needed the capacity to use symbols, tell stories, and make analogies.

When do we first see evidence of that figurative capacity—as well as the other conditions? Until recent findings changed the chronology, it had been common to point to grave goods, personal adornment, and cave art in the Upper Paleolithic period, or Old Stone Age, and argue that the ability to use symbols appeared suddenly between 40,000 and 50,000 years ago. Although the capacity for religion certainly had emerged by then, a few earlier behavioral milestones widen the scope to other *Homo* species and push back the timetable hundreds of thousands of years. Hominins applied natural pigment to decorate bodies and caves, and also used red ochre in the disposal of remains, as early as 300,000 years ago. And some date the first incontestable signs of symbolic thought to that time. In a *Homo heidelbergensis* burial in a deep Spanish sinkhole, excavators found a funerary gift—a pink hand axe—thrown in with the human remains. Even more signs of what scholars call "metaphysical anguish" appear in more purposeful burials later, in Neanderthal and *Homo sapiens* graves in Europe and Central Asia a little less than 100,000 years ago. All human populations were using symbols by then, and scholars of the distant past find symbolically mediated communication among *Homo sapiens* in the incised red ochre, shell beads, and painted images in Blombos Cave on the western cape of South Africa 75,000 years ago.

Signs of nonliteral communication and symbolic action appeared quite early, then, but the excavated traces of religion really start to accumulate in the archaeological record of *Homo sapiens* after 40,000 years ago. By 30,000 years ago, *Homo sapiens* were the only surviving member of the wider human family, and their symbolic communication, moral norms, and ritual action had helped strengthen the bonds of those small hunter-gatherer groups, and probably even afforded them an evolutionary advantage. Our ancestors had built cultural niches in varied ecological settings in Africa, Europe, and Asia that allowed for greater innovation and cooperation than other primates.

So we could start the story of *Homo sapiens* religion at many sites after that moment of cultural evolution. To find early signs of worry and wonder, we can turn to the plains of modern Russia, where two children were interred in a long shallow grave that dates to about 26,000 years ago: a boy and girl covered with red ochre, or hematite, the natural pigment also found at Blombos and many other Paleolithic sites. The mourners also adorned the pair with an extraordinary array of grave goods, including five thousand perforated ivory beads, hundreds of perforated fox teeth, and ivory animal carvings. Or we could point to early cave art, which shows foragers' animal ceremonialism. They imagined wild animals as spirits to be engaged. Just as intriguing, however, are the dozens of portable human figurines, mostly female, found from Italy to Siberia, including the so-called Venus of Willendorf, who was unearthed in present-day Austria. Hunter-gatherers had carved that five-inch limestone image of a mature woman about 25,000 years ago. The ochre-covered image, which was small enough to be carried in one hand, had enlarged breasts and wide hips like later fertility goddesses. She also had a large belly that might have signaled either the effects of longevity or the promise of abundance. Whether those foragers associated the figurine with the generative power of birth or the sustaining gift of food, it almost certainly served a religious purpose. She was a goddess, ancestor, or spirit who played some role in the community's stories, and they appealed to her spiritual power to bring good things or guard against bad things. And everyone needed protection in those precarious times. Subsistence was a struggle. Men and boys hunted wild animals. Women did dangerous, back-breaking work. Babies—and sometimes mothers—died during childbirth.

Shamans played a central role in the religious system that responded to worry as well as wonder, and one shamanic burial in the Near East offers more clues about foraging religion. That 12,000-year-old grave of a petite elderly woman at Hilazon Tachtit is in a funerary cave about eight miles from the Mediterranean in modern Israel. Excavators found evidence of ritual feasting on wild cattle and tortoises, and they unearthed a large number of grave goods—not only red ochre, but also fifty complete tortoise shells and the body parts of local and distant animals, including a wild boar, an eagle, and a leopard. In fact, that woman's elaborate grave, archaeologists suggest, was one of the earliest burials of a shaman. So we can begin the broader narrative of global religion at that cave or at those other sites in South Africa, Russia, or

Austria where those who dug graves, painted rock, and sculpted figurines lived in small itinerant bands that followed the food, seasonally picking plants and tracking game. They probably imagined the wild animals they pursued as superhuman spirits, as we can see from the painted narratives left in caves and the animal parts left in graves. And they seemed to focus on infrequent and highly emotional rituals, like the communal feasts that celebrated a successful hunt or memorialized a spiritual guide.

However, after that cave burial 12,000 years ago, communal lifeways—and spiritual life—began to change.

From foraging to farming religion

The transition from Paleolithic animal symbolism and food-finding to Neolithic food-growing and agricultural imagery was sporadic. Already underway by about 10,000 years ago, or 8000 BCE, that transition occurred independently in at least seven global regions. Early cultivators in the Near East were growing wheat by 9000 BCE, and about the same time other experimental foragers were beginning to plant leren, a potato-like crop, in Las Vegas—no, not that one, but the ancient settlement in southwestern Ecuador. And if we adjusted the timetable and changed the crop, we could add stories about other early planters and plants in Mesoamerica, the Andes, New Guinea, and Asia. Rice cultivation appeared in India, Southeast Asia, and China by 6000 BCE, for example. The new agricultural lifeway spread at different times and in different ways. Where itinerant or semi-sedentary hunter-gatherers were introducing small-scale cultivation, the process was slower; where large-scale tilling and herding were imposed by invading colonizers, the change happened more quickly.

The Neolithic Era in the Near East seems to have been brought on by a convergence of climatic, religious, and social changes. The cultivation of plants and the domestication of animals appeared after the climate changes at the end of the Ice Age. The warmer and wetter conditions transformed the maritime and terrestrial ecology. Sea levels rose, land masses submerged, and forests expanded. Vegetation grew along river valleys, as in the region along the Tigris and Euphrates Rivers known as the Fertile Crescent, where locals began to intentionally cultivate wild grains like wheat and barley. Religion played a role in that transition too. The convening of ceremonies and the construction of architecture fostered the social differentiation and shared identity needed in larger sedentary populations dependent on farming. In particular, communal ritual feasting and labor-intensive monument-building created social bonds within hunter-gatherer bands, but those performative and material expressions of religion also could create even broader group identities in larger farming communities where residents did not all know each other.

But the new utilitarian tools (plows and grinding stones) did not appear suddenly, and neither did the new figurative tools (agricultural metaphors and harvest festivals). To trace the gradual transition from food-gathering religion to food-producing religion, we might look at Jericho, the Jordan Valley site with a tower that was built by early farmers around 8000 BCE, but let's consider a late-Paleolithic site and a Neolithic site in Anatolia or Asia Minor, near the Fertile Crescent. Southern Turkey's Göbekli Tepe (9600–8200 BCE) provides an early example of monumental architecture constructed by foragers. That hilltop ritual site displayed carved symbolic animals on the two hundred limestone pillars that were arranged in twenty circles. Animal symbolism persisted in that semi-sedentary community, even if the structure's construction and ornamentation foreshadowed some aspects of the social life of an agricultural community that would appear later about 250 miles west of Göbekli Tepe.

The thirty-two-acre village of Çatalhöyük in Anatolia offers an interesting example of an early farming settlement (7400–6500 BCE) that retained hunting practices and animal imagery—wild bulls and leopards—while also planting wheat and beans. That

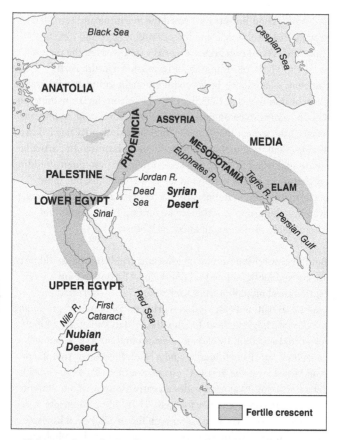

Religion

8. This map shows the Fertile Crescent, a region along the Tigris and
Euphrates Rivers, where ancient residents began to cultivate wild
grains, and Anatolia in present-day Turkey, where there is
monumental architecture constructed by foragers at Göbekli Tepe as
well as the early farming settlement of Çatalhöyük.

72

relatively small and homogeneous community on the floodplain of the Çarşamba River lived in a hive of contiguous units made of sun-dried bricks, which residents entered by a ladder from the roof, a bit like the pueblos of the American Southwest. Çatalhöyük villagers retained the shamanic-centered ritual and art that had characterized the Paleolithic period. They crafted human and animal figurines, and placed animal horns, including those of bulls, in the walls. They also pictured wild animals on the murals that decorated their dwellings and shrines. But we also see home burials more characteristic of sedentary Neolithic farmers. At Çatalhöyük's House B60, for example, mourners interred a young mother who died around 6500 BCE, with the skull of her full-term baby still lodged in the birth canal. The burials continued, but that early farming community's ritual life changed, though it is impossible to say whether those religious changes prompted the lifeway transition or creatively adapted to it. In any case, scholars studying Çatalhöyük have found that as agriculture and domestication intensified, residents' rituals also became more frequent but less emotional. Ritual life was being routinized, and even though shamans would play a role in some early states, as in Shang China, new kinds of ritual specialists, priests, came to be the main presiders at the stationary devotional centers in small-scale farming or herding villages and, later, in agriculturally supported towns, cities, and empires.

Small-scale farming continued in hamlets across the globe, and agriculture did not lead inevitably to urban sprawl and imperial states. Yet intensive farming in complex societies did have epoch-changing religious and social consequences, as in four river valley civilizations that flourished between 3500 and 2000 BCE: along the Nile in Egypt, the Indus in present-day Pakistan and northwestern India, the Tigris and Euphrates in Iraq, and the Yellow River in China. In religious life, cultivators produced more elaborate sacred art and architecture and convened larger communal rituals. Growing seasons regulated farmers' ritual life, and the residential stability that came with agriculture facilitated the growth of religio-political institutions that could transmit communal guidelines. Eventually, in cultures with a writing system, conceptualizing or systematic religious reflection appeared, as agricultural surplus freed up time for spiritual specialists. Although Islam's holy book came later, some important texts associated with the major religious traditions were composed or compiled in complex agricultural societies between 1000 BCE and 200 CE, including the *Rigveda* (1400–1000 BCE), the five Confucian classics (1000–250 BCE), the Prophetic books of the Bible (after 750 BCE), the *Upaniṣads* (600 BCE), the *Lunyu* (Analects) of Kongzi or Confucius (third century BCE), the *Daodejing*, attributed to Daoism's founder Laozi (third century BCE), the Pāli Buddhist canon (first century BCE), the four canonical Christian Gospels (65–95 CE), and the *Mengzi* (second century CE), a Confucian text. Even if some of these very different texts challenged the contemporary social situation—the *Daodejing* called for a return to an earlier age—they all employed the agricultural metaphors that emerged from everyday life, as with Jesus's Parable of the Sower (Mark 4:1–20), the *Daodejing*'s notion of the *dao* as the "root" of all things (chapter 16), and Mengzi's talk of the "sprouts" of moral virtue (2A6, 6A7).

Intensive agriculture also had transforming effects on social life in those valleys, and in other places. Over time, the local populations swelled. And because increasing numbers of people needed to live where crops were planted, processed, and distributed, more and more gathered in and around cities. That higher residential density increased the chance of disease, since infection could spread more easily. The residents of those farming towns and cities were less healthy. Cultivation did allow some food security— they produced the calories their Paleolithic ancestors sought—but, as an analysis of their bones tells us, the diet of agriculturalists often was insufficiently diverse and lacking in protein and vitamins. There were also unintended ecological consequences, like deforestation and soil erosion, as farmers modified the landscape by clearing fields, moving earth, and redirecting

Religion

streams. The Egyptians, for instance, diverted water from the Nile using irrigation ditches, dams, and canals, but sometimes that meant neighbors had less water. And if a farming town abandoned hunting and gathering, or focused too much on a single crop, weather changes or insect infestation could bring nutritional stress, even famine. Harvesting crops—as well as constructing enormous sacred spaces—also required political centralization and labor management. A division of labor assigned tasks and classified people. That social differentiation meant that some did the least valued work. Stratification, even stifling hierarchy, crept in. That social inequity, when combined with residential density, sometimes heightened intracommunal conflict, and where the rulers of the agriculture-based state extended their authority and created an empire it brought interstate warfare.

Ancient religious empires, 550 BCE–476 CE

Neither farming nor farming religion *caused* the rise of empires, but the entwining of political power and religious symbols in a state with cultivated surplus sustained imperial regimes. All four of those river valley civilizations—Egyptian, Mesopotamian, Harappan, and Chinese—affirmed what scholars call divine kingship, the notion that the ruler has a mandate from heaven or a mission from the gods. Early imperial rulers repurposed the older foraging religion and the more recent farming religion to meet new political ends. They began to use religious symbols and myths to centralize power and conquer peoples on a new scale. As the subjugators and the subjugated learned in Archaemenian Persia (550–331 BCE), the largest empire before Rome emerged (246 BCE–476 CE), religion was remarkably well suited to the imperial task. Cyrus the Great founded that empire, and we know a little about what he thought because he left royal inscriptions, like one from 539 BCE that began in Old Persian, "I am Cyrus, King of the World . . . ," and went on to list his fourteen other titles. Cyrus and his successors were not shy. That is because they understood their Archaemenian Empire, which stretched from

Egypt to India, as a religious undertaking on behalf of "the Wise Lord," Ahura Mazdā, the Iranian deity who would become the central (good) god of the Zoroastrian tradition. As the inscriptions show, the rulers appealed to sacred stories about the beginning and end of the world. The Wise Lord had created a "wondrous" world, but things later went wrong. The emperor, inscriptions declared, was chosen by the creator to save the world and restore the earth's original perfection at the end of history. So imperial subjects needed to follow the emperor's commands and perform the required rituals, especially the daily sacrifices, to help bring on this new world. That loyalty and those rites would help the ruler defend "truth" (*arta*) against its adversary, "the Lie" (*Drauga*). And, to provide a material sign of progress, in each newly conquered area the emperor ordered servants to build a lush walled garden, which anticipated the "paradise" (*paridaida*) that was to come.

Well, predictably, paradise did not come. The Persian Empire was overthrown 220 years later by the army of Alexander of Macedon, who had his own imperial ambitions, but other ancient and medieval empires would repeat the Archaemenian pattern, even if the agricultural technology, royal language, and justifying god would change. Two years after Alexander's death, the Mauryan Empire (321–181 BCE) was founded in India. But when the horrific Kalinga war waged by the emperor Aśoka (r. 269–232 BCE) killed and displaced thousands, it left the ruler repentant, as we know from royal inscriptions on pillars, cave walls, and rocks. He scattered those public messages written in Greek, Aramaic, and Prakrit (the vernacular language) around the Indian subcontinent. Aśoka hoped to prevent his descendants from starting other imperial wars. He urged future rulers, and all his subjects, to "consider moral conquest the only true conquest," as Rock Edict 13 put it. After his change of heart, he sent Buddhist emissaries to spread the dharma, the Buddha's spiritual and moral teaching, and waged no other wars to extend the empire. Aśoka's Rock Edict 12 even urged peacefulness toward non-Buddhists: "The faiths of others all deserve to be honored . . . ," that inscription read, "by honoring them, one exalts one's own faith."

Medieval religious empires, 400–1500

A few centuries later, beleaguered Christians in the Roman Empire might have welcomed Aśoka's spirit as they tried to survive periodic persecutions. More like the Archaemenian Empire under Cyrus than the Mauryan Empire under Aśoka, Rome had its imperial gods too. Citizens were expected to give homage to the gods of the state or, during some reigns, risk torture and death. The emperor Constantine, who was more sympathetic to Christianity, came to power in 306 and became convinced by 312 that the Christian faith had offered his army supernatural protection. One of Constantine's successors, Theodosius, went further. He made Christianity the official religion of the Roman Empire in 395. "Pagan" peoples across Europe would contest Christian rule in the following centuries, but the union of the imperial and the spiritual continued, as when Pope Leo III crowned Charlemagne emperor in 800. And by 1000 Christianity, along with Buddhism and Islam, had expanded geographically. Buddhism became the state religion in China's Tang dynasty (618–906), though Neo-Confucianism would dominate during the Song (960–1279). In Nara, Japan's early imperial capital, the emperor dedicated an enormous temple, Tōdaiji, in 752, and that site housed the administrative offices for all Buddhists on the islands. Japan would remain a predominantly Buddhist state until the modern era. A Muslim empire dominated by the caliphs, or successors of Muhammad, also emerged from 632 to 1258, and during that era Islamic rule was established in Cordoba. That Iberian city was "the brilliant ornament of the world," one Christian nun suggested, and a place where Jews and Christians, as "People of the Book," had legal standing.

In the agricultural states of the medieval and early modern world, there were some instances of peaceful coexistence and interreligious conversation, but more moments of conflict, even violence. Francis of Assisi visited Egypt, where he crossed battle lines to talk with Sultan al-Kāmil in 1219, and later in the thirteenth century a Flemish friar inspired by that encounter participated in a debate farther east in the Mongol imperial capital of Qaraquorum. The Mongols, who had a vast empire during the thirteenth century, practiced shamanic divination and ancestor worship, but most of the rulers, or khans (*qaghan*), were pragmatically open to faiths that promised aid in this life or the next. The Mongol court welcomed Nestorian Christians, who had separated from the Latin-speaking church, as well as Buddhists and Muslims. Friar William of Rubruck engaged all those faiths in Qaraquorum, where he participated in a memorable Muslim-Nestorian-Buddhist debate in 1254. The Western Christian reported, as might be expected, that he won the verbal sparring. That did not seem to change the Mongol leader's ideas about global domination, however. When William left in July, the Great Khan gave him a letter for King Louis that instructed the monarch to submit and recognize the Christian state's subordinate place in the Mongol's world empire. Dialogue did not help much, it seems, but at least no one took up arms during the debate.

We cannot say the same about Christian-Muslim-Jewish relations around the world between 1095, when Pope Urban II announced the First Crusade, and 1492, when Christian monarchs expelled Jews and Muslims from Spain. After Muslim colonial expansion had reached Jerusalem and the lands they both called "holy," Islamic and Christian combatants who were promised spiritual reward fought a protracted series of battles. The Muslims who died fighting the infidels would gain paradise, and Christians who took up the sword could expect their reward too, as the sculptural program and liturgical music at Chartres Cathedral made clear. The sculpture portrayed two Crusader saints, St. Eustace and St. George, and *Interni festi gaudia*, a twelfth-century song performed at Chartres and in the Holy Land, praised the Crusades and lifted up those soldiers as moral exemplars. It ended by imploring Jesus, who was addressed as "O unique Emperor":

"Make Christians increase in strength / and the impious waste away / so that the entire kingdom may be subdued / by your almighty power."

Modern religious empires, 1500–1750

Meanwhile, during the last centuries of the Age of Agriculture, the domain of Islam (*Dār al-Islām*) continued to grow as Muslims planted more empires, including the Ottoman Turks (1412–1918), the Safavids of Persia (1500–1779), and the Mughals of India (1526–1730), where the seventeenth-century ruler Shāh Jahān, self-declared "king of the world," commissioned the Taj Mahal as a majestic white marble tomb for his favorite wife. Catholics could brag about Rome's St. Peter's Basilica, also completed in the seventeenth century, but both Catholics and Protestants turned their attention to the task of expanding the domain of Christianity, or Christendom. More precisely, before and after Europe's Age of Religious Wars (1559–1689) Protestant and Catholic empires used new seafaring technology and time-worn political theology to compete not only with Buddhist states and Muslim empires, but also with their fellow Christians as they sailed for Asia and the Americas. The Portuguese Catholic mariner Vasco da Gama reached India in 1500; John Cabot, an Italian navigator commissioned by England, discovered a route across the North Atlantic in 1496; and Christopher Columbus, sailing for Spain, made his way to the Caribbean in 1492.

Columbus, who started colonizing Native Peoples the next year, saw himself as a crusader of sorts. He signed letters "Christ-bearer" and believed he was continuing the Spanish monarchy's campaign to confront and convert non-Christians. He was bringing Christ to the heathen in the Americas. And between 1500 and 1750, European oceanic empires competed for souls and soil. In a variation of the ancient Archaemenian approach, European rulers and officials baptized their colonial campaign in the name of Christianity. Their king had been called by God, and the colonized, they said, were culturally inferior and spiritually imperiled. They were destined for hell. It was the ruler's Christian duty to bring them Christ's saving message—as well as Europe's superior (agricultural) civilization. Most early modern monarchs and missionaries seemed to sincerely believe that, but colonization had tragic consequences, intended and unintended. The colonizers unwittingly spread disease as they transferred biota—not only seedlings and sperm, but germs as well. They also violently displaced peoples, Indigenous and African. In the Americas, those religiously sanctioned colonial processes began with Columbus and continued in colonies governed by the Catholic Spanish, Portuguese, and French, as well as the Protestant English, Danish, and Dutch.

Native displacement and decimation accelerated in the Aztec ceremonial center in the Valley of Mexico and the Incan ceremonial center in the Andes, where there had been great agricultural states for centuries. When Hernán Cortés arrived in Tenochtitlán in 1519 and Francisco Pizarro marched into Cuzco in 1533, colonizers were meeting colonizers in those high-altitude capital cities. Like the Spanish Catholics, both the Aztecs and the Incas had conquered peoples and established religiously figured interaction spheres where outlying political units paid tribute and sent crops to the capital. They both used a capital-centered civic religion, legitimated by cherished myths and elaborate rites, to justify the tribute, control the territories, and unify the worldviews. European-Indigenous encounters in both capitals started with Native attempts to establish alliances by exchanging goods and mates, but that did not work. Imperial representatives had come with the Bible and the plow because they wanted to introduce religion (which the locals already had) and agriculture (which they had too, even earlier than most Europeans). Discoveries of gold and silver in the world they called "new" prompted heightened interest in extractive economies. But as the Native population was decimated by violence and disease, the Spanish—and other Christian colonizers—began to replace forced Indigenous labor in the mines and on the plantations with enslaved Africans. By the time the crossings stopped, about 12.5 million Africans had been forcibly deported, with ports such as Liverpool serving as nodes in the transatlantic network that included complicit African traders who transported locals captured in wars or raids.

As isolated settler outposts in the Americas gradually became interconnected imperial provinces, a crisis of sustainability flared up; between 1650 and 1750, empires' emissaries sanctioned that displacement and enslavement. The English colony of Barbados, for example, became a global sugar producer by 1680, and the average plantation had eighty slaves working in brutal conditions. On the island and back in London, a few religiously inspired dissenters spoke out, but the imperial church and state mostly made things worse. Throughout this period some Protestant and Catholic leaders continued to preach a gospel of equality, but most European newcomers did little to defend Native Peoples, resist African slavery, or restore damaged niches.

The colonial crisis would remain unresolved as stressed spaces like the mission and the plantation became increasingly unsustainable, since export agriculture and merchant capitalism depended on forced labor and inequitable distribution. The European imperial competition, being fought in Africa and Asia as well as the Americas, would continue until a global conflict between Protestant and Catholic empires called the Seven Years' War started in 1756. It would be the last of the religious wars, but, since it involved every continent and all major European states, it also would be the first *world* war. As empires clashed, the effects were felt from India to America. If you were keeping score—and everyone was—Protestant Britain gained the most. Yet the victor's American colonies soon would seek the sanction of "Nature's God" for a rebellion that would lead, by the end of the Revolutionary War, to the rise of a new nation-state—and a vigorous form of the religious nationalism that continues to shape the world today. That new form of political organization, the nation, would be key after 1789, and especially between 1840 and 1940, when global migrations changed societies and the Industrial Age supplanted the Agricultural Age.

From agricultural to industrial religion

The first big factory building, England's Derby Silk Mill, opened in 1721, but the shift from growing crops to manufacturing products—and the move from mercantile to industrial capitalism—really started in a rural village near Manchester, England, in 1784, when an Ulster-born Protestant founded Quarry Bank Mill. That cotton mill, which got its first raw material from the Caribbean and its first child workers from the poorhouse, sat at the confluence of two streams, and it used a water wheel to power new spinning machines to manufacture yarn. By 1816 its 252 employees were producing almost 350,000 pounds of yarn each year. Cotton was not new. It was mentioned in the *Rigveda* and grown or imported in early empires from the Indus Valley to the Andes. But for the first time a water-powered machine was transforming the fluffy white fiber into profitable finished cloth. Soon more efficient machines would use steam power, and, as the nineteenth century went on, the steam engine would power ships and trains as it also mechanized production. Coal would fuel this First Industrial Revolution, but religion nudged it along too, as most spiritual leaders embraced this lifeway change and factories—and factory religion—spread to continental Europe, the United States, and Japan by 1900.

This transition, like the shift to farming, was complicated. The perplexing question of why an industrial revolution began in England and not, for example, in China has preoccupied countless interpreters. There have been almost as many theories as theorists. Some explanations focus on material, ecological, or psychological factors. One account suggests that it had to do with the individualistic psychology produced by European wheat farming, which could be done by a single person or family, as opposed to the collectivist psychology generated by Chinese rice farming, which required communal cooperation. Those individualistic wheat farmers, the argument goes, were more inclined to the innovation that led to the new industrial technologies. Other interpreters have pointed to religious differences. It was Protestantism, they say, with its emphasis on the ordinary believer's ability to interpret scripture, that empowered the individual and cultivated the self-discipline that led to the rise of a merchant class of prosperous Protestants in port cities like London. That religiously inspired commercial revolution, these interpreters suggest, created the capitalists ready to invest in the new factories. We can't settle this long debate here and must only conclude that multiple factors, including religious ones, were at work.

Fortunately, there is more agreement about the social and ecological effects of the Industrial Revolution. Population density grew even more. Housing and health worsened for the rural migrants who moved from farms to factories. That meant even more exposure to disease, and the city dwellers' descendants were also less equipped to deal with germs. Farmers' exposure to microbes through daily contact with dirt had immunized them from some illnesses, but later generations lost that protection in the industrial city. And those cities got bigger. So did the gap between the poor and the rich. The economic and social hierarchy put industrial capitalists at the top and wage workers at the bottom. The pace of life changed too. Humans managed time in a new way. It was no longer determined by seasonal shifts or the sun's rising and setting, as it was for farmers. Factory bells now rang to signal the start and end of days, and workers had to keep up with the speed of the machines and the needs of the market. That is one reason the Japanese started to buy Western time pieces, clocks for homes and pocket watches for managers, just as the nation started to industrialize. Finally, industrialization also had its visible and invisible ecological consequences. Many contemporaries commented on the grime of coal-powered factory towns, but we now know what they did not—that by the 1830s the release of carbon dioxide and other greenhouse gases had begun to slowly warm the earth. So climate change, as well as economic disparity, originated with the human-made effects of the Industrial Revolution.

The rise of industry did not mean the demise of religion. Friedrich Engels, the atheist coauthor of the *Communist Manifesto* (1848), suggested in his earlier study of the English working class that religion was dying out. But that prediction proved wrong, or at least incomplete, as did later forecasts during the 1960s. Religion has not gone away in our century, and it did not go away with the rise of industrialization in the 1800s.

The situation did change, however, and some changes invigorated religion, at least as it was practiced by the elite and the middling classes. Global historians have suggested that the nineteenth century saw a reemergence and expansion of religion around the world. Aggressive European Christian empires and insurgent non-European states promoted religion as a source of their unifying identity, as ancient empires had done. Global religious institutions also consolidated—not only the Catholic Church, with its increasingly Vatican-centered devotion, but also groups of Hindus, Buddhists, Muslims, and Protestants, who benefitted from the advances in transportation and communication. Faster railroad and steamship transportation allowed those of the same faith to collaborate, and those who wanted to persuade nonbelievers could reach them more quickly. After 1844 the telegraph allowed faster communication. The first telegraph message quoted the Bible—"What hath God wrought"—and globalizing religious networks took advantage of the "miracle" of the age. In August 1858, Queen Victoria of Britain sent a message to US president James Buchanan across a new underwater cable, and reactions on both sides of the Atlantic used religious language to herald a new age of international cooperation. One New York newspaper attributed the invention to "the directing hand of

Providence," and predicted it would "accelerate the wheels of progress." Further, as "the Great Peacemaker," the telegraph would eliminate wars caused by misunderstanding. That didn't happen, but the telegraph, along with inexpensive print culture and improved mail delivery, did allow middle-class adherents around the world to read magazine articles and books about their own and other faiths. Using translations that appeared by mid-century, for example, English speakers from Bombay to Boston could decide for themselves about the Bible, the Qurʾān, the Gītā, and some Buddhist texts. They even could find a translation of Aśoka's rock inscriptions, which led some spiritually disillusioned Americans and Europeans between 1880 and 1900 to conclude that Buddhism was better than Christianity at encouraging peaceful interactions among nations.

Hindu gurus from India and Buddhist priests from Japan agreed about Christianity's defects, and they joined others on the move to cross the globe by 1900 to promote their traditions, including at Chicago's World's Parliament of Religions in 1893. Protestant missionaries from Europe and America also went just about everywhere a steamship or train could take them. There were round-trip spiritual journeys too, like the increased number of Muslim pilgrims who could travel to Mecca. The new transportation technologies also allowed unprecedented global migrations, and the transplanted carried their faiths and blended them with the dominant religion of their adopted homelands. Pushed by famine, religious persecution, or political unrest—and pulled by the promise of a better life—about 73 million Europeans and 22 million Chinese left home between 1840 and 1940, and those migrants diversified religious life where they settled, including in New York, Singapore, and Buenos Aires.

The modern industrial world did allow some wage laborers to sleep in on Sundays, as Engels hoped, but there were multiple ways of being modern, and most of them used religion to celebrate the factory, even if some spiritually minded reformers criticized its social effects. Industrialists around Manchester, the center of the First Industrial Revolution, viewed piety as an ally, not just for themselves but also for their employees. Managers and ministers exalted virtues promoted by the churches and necessary for factory life—punctuality, self-discipline, and frugality. In other words, they attended to religion and to the factory's "moral economy," as one British advocate put it. That meant monitoring what laborers did in the dormitory as well as on the factory floor, and it meant encouraging or requiring religious worship. Samuel Greg, who built Quarry Bank Mill in the rural village of Styal and owned a townhouse in nearby Manchester, circulated a list of moral infractions and corresponding fines, and in 1822 he built a Baptist chapel near Quarry Bank Mill, even though he was raised a Presbyterian and had converted to Unitarianism, a denomination that rejected Jesus's divinity and emphasized his moral teaching. A number of Greg's workers were Baptists, so he provided a space for worship, just as he also encouraged the child laborers living in his dormitories to attend the local Anglican parish church.

That "moral machinery" hummed and rattled in other industrial towns too. On both sides of the Atlantic, for example, wage workers "got religion" at Methodist-led revivals or got assistance at Unitarian-led "benevolent societies." Factory workers in industrializing Łódź, then part of the Russian Empire, used Catholicism, Protestantism, and Judaism not only for psychic comfort but also to make things better through individual self-help, neighborly support, or political action. The owners of the first silk factories and cotton mills in late nineteenth-century Japan highlighted the link between the imperial state and Shintō, which imagined the emperor as divine. As seen in the lyrics of one song sung at a Japanese silk factory, manufacturers suggested work at the loom meant support for the empire: "Reel, reel the thread / Thread is the treasure of the empire!" There were even more systematic efforts in Lowell, Massachusetts, America's first factory town, where a local Unitarian minister talked about the factory's "moral machinery" as he championed the water-powered cotton mills that opened in 1826. Lowell, he pointed out, boasted supervised women's boarding houses, posted lists of moral rules, and constructed lots of Christian churches, including one sponsored by the textile corporation. But factory religion was not just top-down. As the diaries and letters of Lowell's female workers confirm, there was a surprising spiritual vitality and diversity in early industrializing cities.

For the first time, in 1850, more residents lived in towns than in the countryside in Britain, and by 1900 there were signs of a shift to industrialization and urbanization in the United States and western Europe. However, the great divergence between the North Atlantic world and Asia had widened dramatically. Outside of Japan, Asia still had little industry, and only 4 percent of the population in China and 11 percent in India lived in cites by then. But the Western lifeway transition also meant a shift from an organic to a mineral economy, and global coal production started to rise by 1850. Oil production would spike after 1920. The early nineteenth-century habitat had relied on the capture of solar energy, as farming communities had for a long time. The sun's energy drove rain and wind patterns that generated wind for sails and falling water for mills. Plants, including the trees used as firewood for homes, steamboats, and factories, depended on the sun to grow. The emerging mineral niche, which intensively used fossil fuels, also relied indirectly on the solar energy that had produced hydrocarbons from the remains of plants and animals over millions of years. And some proponents of "natural theology" in Britain, which had a head start on extracting coal and sanctifying industry, suggested that God had created the conditions for coal to emerge in the Carboniferous Period about 300 million years ago. In other words, God made coal—and, indirectly, the new industrial habitat, which would depend first on coal and then on oil.

It happened at different times, but folks in the industrializing world found themselves becoming dependent on new energy sources as the First Industrial Revolution used water and steam power to mechanize manufacturing, and the Second used electric power to create mass production. To explain this onset of fossil-fuel dependency, some specialists have talked about the "momentum" of technological change, or the "infrastructure trap" in the built environment. But the language we have used about making and breaking niches also captures this process. In these terms, the West's religiously inflected habitat was transitioning from an agricultural to an industrial niche.

Even though the technological innovations—and environmental impacts—were unevenly distributed in the "developed" and "developing" worlds, the new energy economies generated changes in daily life that would have global effects between 1840 and 1945. In short, the "wheels of progress" did not always run smoothly. New kinds of empires enriched by industrial capitalism sent missionaries to "civilize" and "convert" the heathen in Africa and Asia as a new era of religiously sanctioned colonialism began. One of the most famous British missionaries, Dr. David Livingstone, was diverted from his original goal of saving the Chinese and sailed for Africa instead. The Congregationalist preacher and medical doctor arrived in Cape Town in 1841, and he would spend thirty years in southern, central, and eastern Africa extoling the new industrial age and promising that colonialism, commerce, and Christianity would bring people together. "The tendency and spirit of the age are more and more towards the undertaking of industrial enterprises," Livingstone wrote in one of his last journals, and "the extension and use of railroads, steamships, telegraphs, break down nationalities and bring peoples geographically remote into close connection commercially and politically. They make the world one, and capital, like water, tends to a common level." Not all of the colonized, including Christian converts, agreed that there was economic leveling and that things were coming together. In fact, as the Nigerian writer Chinua

Achebe suggested in his 1958 novel *Things Fall Apart*, Christian missionaries and colonial officials destroyed Igbo communal life in Nigeria, the West African land that got missionaries in the 1880s and became a British protectorate in 1901. Missionaries destabilized the religious system that supported the local grazing and farming culture, and, as one character in *Things Fall Apart* observes, that had sad consequences: "All our gods are weeping."

There would be other sources of grief—and signs of things coming apart—during the first half of the twentieth century. Racism surged during the 1920s, a depression struck during the 1930s, and capitalist and socialist nations that shared a faith in factories but disagreed about faith in God waged two world wars. Industrial nations were among the combatants; and religion—and anti-religion—played a role. Long-standing divisions among Orthodox, Catholic, and Muslim communities on Europe's Balkan Peninsula grew into a global struggle among nation-states on St. Vitus Day in 1914. The Balkans had been freed from Ottoman Muslim rule the year before, so that Serbian Orthodox holy day commemorating Christians killed by Muslims in the Battle of Kosovo (1389) had heightened meaning. But the South Slav people who affiliated with the Orthodox Church still did not enjoy autonomy, since the Catholic Austro-Hungarian monarchy had recently annexed land in the Balkans. To destabilize that monarchy and unite South Slav peoples, a Bosnian-born atheist, whom the Serbian Orthodox Church would later honor as a "hero," assassinated the Catholic heir to the Austrian throne on that holy day in 1914. That started a war which reached beyond southeastern Europe and included industrial powers like Britain, America, and Germany.

The First World War also ended on St. Vitus Day, with the signing of the Paris peace treaty in 1919, and two years later on that same day on the Serbian Orthodox calendar the constitution for a new Slav kingdom, later called Yugoslavia, took effect. Farther east, in lands where the Russian Orthodox Church had historic influence,

Joseph Stalin succeeded the socialist revolutionary Vladimir Lenin as leader of the Soviet Union in 1924, and that dictator transformed the atheist state into an industrial power that fought beside Western allies in World War II. During that global conflict, stretching from 1939 to 1945, the state religion of Shintō justified Japan's imperial military efforts, and Germany's National Socialist (Nazi) Party affirmed a nonsectarian Christianity, while also pledging to "combat the Jewish-materialistic spirit at home and abroad."

After 1945 the Jews, who lost six million people in the Nazi concentration camps, would get their own state, and so would many former colonies, including Achebe's Nigeria. But that did not bring peace or justice. The postwar period became an atomic age when the United States dropped bombs on Japan to end the conflict, and for some the subsequent Cold War arms race tempered the older exuberance over technological wonders. However, it was still an industrial age, as even more nations, including the People's Republic of China (1949), welcomed big factories, and almost everyone ignored the environmental effects and social costs as they sought access to fossil fuels, including in the increasingly volatile Middle East. In many places in the postwar world, human habitats seemed less sustainable, and by the twenty-first century the religious faced the daunting task of restoring those niches while also negotiating another big lifeway transition.

Chapter 5
Global religion today

It was still unclear after 1945 whether religion—and the nationalist impulses and industrial economies it sometimes sanctioned—was bringing things together or pulling them apart. That question was even harder to answer after the 1970s, when politically assertive religion staged a comeback, global flows intensified, and environmental damage accelerated. It was also a time when silicon microprocessors and utopian spiritual visions facilitated another big transition—from the Industrial Age to the Information Age.

The best available evidence suggests that today more than eight in ten people in the world identify with a religious group. Of those who do, there are about 2.3 billion Christians (31.1 percent of the religious population), about half of them Catholic, and 1.9 billion Muslims (24.9 percent), of whom about 87 percent are Sunni. The 1.1 billion Hindus (15.2 percent) and the more than 500 million Buddhists (6.6 percent) make up the other largest groups of religious adherents today. But about 400 million people (6 percent) practice an Indigenous or "folk" tradition. There are also about 14 million Jews worldwide (.2 percent). Slightly less than 1 percent of the global population (58 million) identify with all of the rest of the religions, including the Bahá'í faith, Daoism, Jainism, Shinto, Sikhism, and Zoroastrianism. For example, there are about 25 million Sikhs, most of them in India, and at least

4 million Jains there too, according to the national census. The Baháʼí faith reports 5 million adherents. Daoists are difficult to count, but one estimate suggests there are about 8 million, mostly in China.

Christianity is the most evenly dispersed tradition, spreading in all directions from its cradle land in Palestine. It is a majority faith in Europe, the Americas, and Australia, and has a major presence in sub-Saharan Africa. Islam, which originated in western Arabia, predominates in a wide swath from western Africa to western Asia. Hinduism, which spread south from its natal region in the Indus Valley, mostly still concentrates in the Asia-Pacific region, and Buddhism spread into South and East Asia from its origin near the Ganges River in India. Only these four traditions can claim national or regional dominance, though about three-quarters of the world's 1.1 billion "unaffiliated" persons live in the populous Asia-Pacific region. More than half of the residents of China and Japan are "nones," for instance.

The map of the global religious landscape provides a useful overview, but it does not tell the full story. It does not show, for example, the local pluralism that flourishes amid the regional dominance. Buddhism retains some of its historic significance in both Japan, where more than a third of residents affiliate with the tradition, and the People's Republic of China, where more than 18 percent still embrace the Buddha's teachings—even after the Cultural Revolution (1966–76) persecuted adherents and the Chinese state continued to oversee the five officially recognized religions (Buddhism, Daoism, Catholicism, Protestantism, and Islam). The map distorts in another way. It seems to suggest that the unaffiliated are regionally confined to Asia, mostly in socialist states. Yet if we look at the second-largest category, we find that "nones" also have a presence in a number of Christian-majority democratic countries, including Great Britain (27.8 percent), Australia (24.2 percent), the United States (16.4 percent), and Norway (10 percent). Visualizing the religious world in terms of

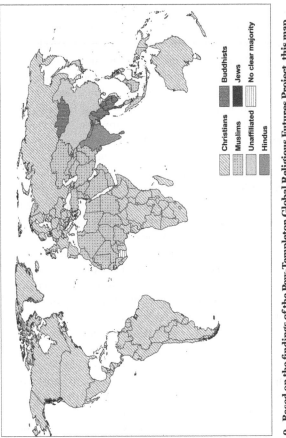

Legend:
- Christians
- Muslims
- Hindus
- Buddhists
- Jews
- Unaffiliated
- No clear majority

9. Based on the findings of the Pew–Templeton Global Religious Futures Project, this map shows the majority religion in each country. It portrays the wide geographical dispersal of Christianity and the regional concentrations of Muslims, Hindus, Buddhists, as well as those who tell researchers they are not affiliated with any religion.

regional dominance also obscures the enduring presence of Indigenous and folk traditions. These traditions predominate in just three countries (Macau, Taiwan, and Vietnam), but they are the second largest in twenty-three others, including China.

The map also obscures change over time. There are 370 million Indigenous people around the world today, but that statistic and this map do not reveal that adherents have been declining because of the impact of religious colonization and missionary activity between 1840 and 1940. In sub-Saharan Africa, for example, the followers of African traditional religions constitute about 7 percent of the contemporary population, but those faiths have been challenged by the stunning regional growth of Christianity and Islam since 1900. Other twentieth-century changes also reconfigured the global religious landscape, including the partitioning of Hindu India and Muslim Pakistan when the Indian subcontinent achieved independence from Britain in 1948. Political borders, like lines on a map, do not always neatly divide religious worlds, however. A substantial Muslim population remains in contemporary India, which now has nine of ten Hindus, but could boast the world's largest Muslim population by 2050. Further, Hindus' presence outside India is also obscured by the mapmakers. There are significant Hindu populations on the nearby island of Sri Lanka (13.6 percent), which has a Muslim and Christian presence too, and, in the Americas, in Trinidad and Tobago (23 percent) and Suriname (19.8 percent).

Finally, nine countries have no clear religious majority. Nigeria, for example, now has almost identical proportions of Christians (49.3 percent) and Muslims (48.4 percent). And no tradition predominates in Asian nations with a continuing Buddhist presence, like Taiwan, South Korea, and Vietnam. In Singapore, one of the receiving nations during the global migrations between 1840 and 1940, Buddhism claims the most adherents (33.9 percent), but sizeable Christian, Muslim, and Hindu populations make its religious landscape remarkably diverse.

Coming together and coming apart, 1945–1975

During the first decades of the postwar period, the unifying forces seemed to be winning. Representatives from dozens of countries formed intergovernmental organizations, such as the World Bank (1944), the International Monetary Fund (1945), and the United Nations (1945), to coordinate economic development and enhance political cooperation. Equally important, even though eight nations abstained—the Soviet bloc, South Africa, and Saudi Arabia—a religiously diverse group that included a Catholic, Confucian, Hindu, and Muslim successfully negotiated the UN's Universal Declaration of Human Rights (1948), which proclaimed that "the inherent dignity" and "equal and inalienable rights of all members of the human family is the foundation of freedom, justice, and peace in the world."

The World Council of Churches, which includes most Protestant and Eastern Orthodox bodies, was organized in Amsterdam in 1948, and by the mid-sixties the Roman Catholic Church, which had condemned modernity, would endorse church-state separation, interreligious dialogue, and humane global development. The Catholic priest Gustavo Gutiérrez was trying to reimagine economic "development" when he proposed his emerging "liberation theology" at a conference in Chimbote, Peru, in the summer of 1968. God, he argued, was on the side of the oppressed. That new approach, which would influence Asia and Africa as well as the Americas, sought to close the gap between the rich and the poor.

There were other gaps to close as well. Feminist theologies championing gender equity emerged at this time, and spiritually inspired movements for civil rights also imagined a more just social order. That happened in the United States, where Christian leaders such as Martin Luther King Jr. pressed for racial justice, and in India, where B. R. Ambedkar, a Buddhist convert and former untouchable, challenged the caste system and became the chief draftsman of the nation's new constitution. Like India, former colonies in the Americas, Asia, and Africa became autonomous nations between the 1940s and 1960s. Some were secular states that initially promised civil and religious protections.

The global spread of the factory brought some economic improvement, and new technologies brought people together. The first commercial communication satellite was launched in 1965. Television allowed a large and diverse audience to share common experiences, notably the 1969 moon walk, and NASA's lunar orbiter also provided the first photograph of the whole Earth from space. That image, which pictured humans' shared home, became an icon for the global environmental movement that was taking shape. The first flight of the Boeing 747 jumbo jet took off that same year, making the world even smaller. The world felt smaller for the religious too. Adherents could fly to sacred spaces more quickly, but even believers who stayed home could connect with coreligionists by telephone or tune in to get a televised glimpse of religious pluralism by watching coverage of worshippers praying at the Wailing Wall in Jerusalem or bathing in the sacred waters of the Ganges in Benares.

On the other hand, between 1945 and 1975 things also seemed to be coming apart, and religion was a fragmenting force. Many suggested there were now three worlds: a "First World" of free market nations; a communist "Second World"; and a poorer, nonindustrial but emergent "Third World." First and Second World rivalries dominated the period. In fact, tensions between the "greedy capitalists" of the God-affirming West and the "godless Communists" of the Soviet Union and China brought the world to the brink of nuclear war more than once in the Cold War period, including during the thirteen-day standoff of the 1962 Cuban Missile Crisis. In these years, the decolonizing nations struggled to decide on the place of religion in public life, and clashes among the religious—or between religious and Marxist factions—sparked civil wars or triggered state aggression. On the Indian subcontinent, for example, a Hindu nationalist assassinated Mohandas Gandhi, and it was only the partition dividing Muslim Pakistan and Hindu India that seemed able to temporarily quell interreligious violence.

Chinese troops entered Buddhist Tibet in 1959 and exiled its religious and political leader, Tenzin Gyatso, the Fourteenth Dalai Lama. Religious civil wars were waged in Burma and Cyprus. And during the Six-Day War of 1967, displaced Palestinians and their allies in Muslim-majority nations battled the US-backed Israelis, who expanded their borders by capturing the Gaza Strip and the Sinai Peninsula. In Northern Ireland, the Protestant British enclave established by seventeenth-century colonization and solidified during the dividing of the Catholic South and Protestant North in 1921, erupted into what amounted to a religious civil war in 1968. "The Troubles," as locals called that inter-Christian conflict, would kill almost four thousand people over the next three decades.

During the mid-sixties, weariness at global religious conflict and optimism about proliferating secular states mingled with the widespread perception that religion was—and should be—receding to the private sphere. "Is God Dead?," *Time* magazine's cover story asked in 1966. Some of the war-weary on the ground and many academics on campus said yes—and good riddance. However, few of those prognosticators of secularism were paying attention to Protestant evangelical preachers, who continued to draw crowds at revivals around the world, or to Muslims and Buddhists who were starting to make claims on public space in decolonizing nations. Only slowly did some journalists and scholars notice that young people were not rejecting all religion. They were instead looking back and turning east. By 1968 a global countercultural movement was challenging the Judeo-Christian tradition that participants blamed for creating bloody wars, smokestack pollution, and social inequality. There were socialists whose atheist utopia involved revolution, of course, but many young people, from Portland to Paris, sought spiritual alternatives from Indigenous and Asian traditions. Some traveled to India or Japan to find wisdom. Others set out for the thousands of new utopian communities, where cultural dissenters sought a way of life more attuned to the seasonal rhythms of the farm than the workday whistle of the factory.

Coming together and coming apart, 1976–2007

Pol Pot, the Marxist dictator who led the Khmer Rouge regime in Cambodia in 1976, had agrarian utopian dreams too, though they involved the forced relocation of his people to farming collectives, and—even though he was raised as a Buddhist—he advocated the systematic destruction of Buddhism. As many as 2.5 million Cambodians died by 1979. Soldiers and police officers destroyed one-third of the Buddhist temples, and many monks were killed or exiled. That experience, and a violence-supporting interpretation of a Buddhist text, the *Mahāvaṃsa*, would be remembered in Sri Lanka in 1983, as the minority Hindu Tamils rose up against the ruling Sinhalese Buddhists. Hindus also engaged in interreligious violence that threatened to unravel the social fabric in India, where tensions with Muslims persisted and Sikhs demanded a separate homeland. To contain those Sikh separatists, in 1984 the Indian army attacked one of the most revered of the Sikhs' gurdwaras, the Golden Temple in Amritsar. Continuing the cycle of violence, later that year the Indian prime minister Indira Gandhi was assassinated by her Sikh bodyguards.

Religion and ethnic identity also widened divides during the Balkan Wars (1991–95), when Eastern Orthodox Serbs, Roman Catholic Croats, and Bosnian Muslims displayed sacred symbols as they fought the bloodiest European conflict since World War II. Thanks to the loosening of controls on public religious expression in the former Yugoslavia, all three groups had begun to assert competing claims on civic space in the seventies, and then war broke out after the collapse of the Soviet Union in 1989. By the end of the Balkan conflict, which unleashed terror and rape, Yugoslavia had disintegrated into five successor states. Several million people also had been forcibly resettled, and about 150,000 died, including the Bosnian Muslim victims of genocide in Srebrenica, a preventable tragedy that the UN secretary-general said "will forever weigh on the collective conscience of the international community."

Before that tragedy, Middle Eastern Islam also attracted the attention of the international community. In 1979, the same year that American Protestant televangelist Jerry Falwell formed the "Moral Majority," the exiled cleric Ayatollah Khomeini returned to lead a revolution in the new nation that would be called the Islamic Republic of Iran. After the anti-imperialist revolutionaries deposed the US-backed shah and took American diplomats hostage, Khomeini helped design the blueprint for the new government. It would have an official state religion, Shi'i Islam, and rest ultimate authority in a supreme leader, the "Guardian Jurist," and a Guardian Council of Muslim judges with veto power over legislation.

That new nation would inspire Muslim insurgents around the world, but for Osama bin Laden, who initially had no plans for an Islamic state, it was "infidel" aggression against Muslims in Palestine and Afghanistan that provided motivation. Bin Laden dated his political awakening to the Yom Kippur War of 1973, when Saudi Arabia's King Faisal imposed an oil embargo against the United States and other countries that supported Israel during the fourth Arab-Israeli war. Then, in the 1980s, Bin Laden went to Afghanistan and, with CIA help, set up a guesthouse called Sijill al-Qaeda (Register of the Base) for Arab recruits who would battle the Soviet Union. Emboldened by those rebukes to superpowers and fortified by his austere interpretation of an earlier Muslim reform movement, called Wahhabism, Bin Laden criticized elite fellow Muslims—Shi'i and Sufi, and even "apostate" Sunnis who seemed complicit with the West. In fact, his first public statement in 1994 was a criticism of a Saudi cleric who had endorsed the Oslo Accords, a 1993 agreement between Israel and the Palestine Liberation Organization (PLO). Using language reminiscent of medieval conflicts over the Holy Land, he condemned Saudi cooperation with "the forces of the aggressive Crusader-Jewish alliance." He directed that same pious fury against American "crusaders" as he helped plan the attacks on the World Trade Center on September 11, 2001. US-led coalitions then retaliated with invasions of Iraq and Afghanistan.

If we stopped the story there, the evidence would suggest that things were mostly falling apart. However, over those same decades, adhesive spiritual forces worked for peace and justice. Those forces included small acts of resistance by ordinary people during the Balkan Wars. The Catholic Croat Rudolf Hren refused to leave his Muslim neighbors in Srebrenica, where he later was found in a mass grave. A Jewish family that survived the Nazis during World War II because of a Muslim family, the Hardagas, returned the favor by securing safe passage for their former protectors and three hundred other Muslims who faced genocide. There were also Buddhist attempts at peacebuilding. A decade after the genocide in Pol Pot's Cambodia, a Buddhist monk who lost his entire family and most of his friends began to preach social peace as well inner peace, and in 1992 that monk, Samdech Preah Maha Ghosananda, began to lead peace walks. By then others had begun to practice what Thich Nhat Hanh called "engaged Buddhism." A Vietnamese Buddhist, whom Martin Luther King nominated for the Nobel Peace Prize, Nhat Hanh nonviolently protested the Vietnam War during the sixties, and his friend Suluk Sivaraksa, the Thai author of *A Buddhist Vision for Renewing Society*, helped found the International Network of Engaged Buddhists in 1989. That same year, the exiled Dalai Lama won the Nobel Peace Prize for his insistence that resistance to the Chinese occupation of Tibet must be nonviolent.

After the Rwandan genocide of 1994, Catholic Relief Services began to shift its focus from economic aid and disaster relief to peacebuilding, and the Good Friday Agreement signed by the United Kingdom and the Republic of Ireland in 1998 provided for power-sharing with Catholics, who constituted about 30 percent of the population of Northern Ireland. A few ordinary Catholics and Protestants had prepared the way for the agreement, but the peacebuilding effort in northern Kenya was almost completely a bottom-up initiative. Dekha Ibrahim Abdi and three other Muslim women founded the Wajir Peace and Development Committee in 1993 to reduce violence among pastoralist clans of Kenyan Somalis in that drought-plagued area. Her strategy was so successful that it drew government support and became an international model for peacebuilding.

It makes sense that public attention has focused on religion, conflict, and peacebuilding, but there were other social and spiritual changes between 1976, when Apple Computer was founded and the UN's Environment Programme launched a newsletter called *Connect*, and 2007, when Apple introduced the iPhone and Al Gore and the UN's Intergovernmental Panel on Climate Change (IPCC) won the Nobel Peace Prize. Religion, it turns out, played a role in both the environmental movement and the digital revolution.

The religious link with environmentalism went back to the 1700s, when a Scandinavian Lutheran minister named Peter Kalm helped promote a "green revolution" in early modern Europe by challenging Adam Smith's assumption that capitalist markets and natural ecologies would automatically be brought into balance. Kalm and other early environmentalists insisted that responsible agriculture required careful management of the land and natural resources. The ill effects of industrialization became clear by the middle of the twentieth century, and a new environmental movement began in the 1960s and accelerated by the 1990s, when interfaith groups and religious traditions started to circulate public statements about ecological ethics. By 2003 the World Bank had published a report titled *Faith in Conservation*, which included statements from eleven religions, including Christianity, Buddhism, and Islam. The Muslim contribution, by a Kenyan biologist, suggested that an ecological ethic rests on several principles taken from the Qur'ān, including the ideas that all things in heaven and earth are God's, humans have been appointed as *Khalīfa*, or guardians of nature, and God has commanded believers to "waste not by excess." Christian and Buddhist thinkers offered their own contributions to the global conversation about green religion.

Just as religion supported the late eighteenth-century Industrial Revolution that began in Manchester's bowl-shaped valley a hundred miles southwest of London, it also inspired the digital utopianism of the Information Age that emerged about fifty miles south of San Francisco in a region a journalist dubbed "Silicon Valley." Steve Jobs and Steve Wozniak, who founded Apple there in 1976, were shaped by the egalitarian social ethic and countercultural piety of the sixties. That "techno-mysticism," as some have called it, appropriated multiple non-Christian practices, including ancient Chinese divination, native peyote-induced trance, and Japanese Zen meditation. Jobs explored Hinduism during a seven-month stay in India and diligently practiced Zen meditation in California. The countercultural mix of personal piety and social utopianism found expression in the Whole Earth Network of conferences and publications, including the communalists' Bible, the *Whole Earth Catalog* (1968), which Jobs later described as "Google in paperback form, thirty-five years before Google came along." That magazine and product catalog announced its purpose in recommending not just books for learning but also tools for creating: "We are as gods and might as well get used to it." Humans were called to use tools, both the simple implements of the communalists building Native tipis on farms and the complex machines of the techies assembling computers in garages. Even though mathematicians and defense industry experts played key roles in the rise of the computer, the Information Age's social vision—with its focus on bringing the world together—owed a great deal to countercultural religion, even if the corporate world's quest for earning would compete with the spiritual ethic of sharing.

With the invention of the World Wide Web in 1989 at CERN, a European research facility, and the introduction of Apple's smart phone in 2007, that dream seemed to be becoming a reality. One high-tech CEO suggested that Jobs's unveiling of the iPhone at a developers' conference in California marked the dawn of a new global era: "Six decades into the computer revolution, four decades since the invention of the microprocessor, and two decades into the rise of the modern Internet, all of the technology required to transform industries through software finally works and can be widely delivered at global scale."

The technological shift inspired by countercultural religion affected how religion would be expressed. The new communication technologies provided the pious with new ways to mark time and map space. Digital calendars allowed devotees to download their tradition's sacred calendar, so Hindus could know when to start the five-day festival of Diwali and Muslims could know when to end the month-long fast during Ramaḍān. But temporal orientation involves more than that, as one Silicon Valley engineer who designs calendar software discovered. He was surprised to find that most users' attitudes toward time are "like a whole religion almost." "They come," he explained, "with a set of values on how you should live your life." The religious also come with a sense of where they should be headed, and the Information Age provided new metaphors for the journey. Consider Protestant spiritual guides, a centuries-old literary genre. John Bunyan's 1678 fictional tale, *The Pilgrim's Progress*, traced the dangers that "Christian" faced as he made his way to the "Celestial City." In a similar way, the twenty-first century book *God's GPS for Your Soul II*, by Liberty Savard, mapped the "Highway to Heaven." This evangelical Protestant volume assured Christian travelers that God's GPS, holy scripture, provides clear directions, and even offers "recalculating warnings" when the follower strays from the path.

As this example shows, the networked world provided new ways of *imagining* and industrial metaphors did not disappear, but now there were computer analogies too. And the metaphoric transfer went in both directions—from technology to religion *and* from religion to technology. Choose any form of new media, and you will find that the religious have appropriated technological language for spiritual purposes. This has been true since the telegraph shaped nineteenth-century Spiritualist discourse about communications from the spirit world. Computer analogies began to exert global influence in the 1970s, as worried families talked about hiring cult "de-programmers" to reverse the "programming" their loved ones had received in movements like the Korean-based Unification Church. Those analogies continued as North American social media users began talking about "friending God" and, more recently in India, a Sikh spiritual teacher with mystical inclinations suggested that devotees should "download God." The metaphoric transfer went the other way too. Spiritual referents accompanied the introduction of the iPhone in 2007. Amid the mood of millennial expectation, a blogger sarcastically called it the "Jesus Phone," as if the savior's return was approaching, and more than two dozen newspapers in five countries repeated that phrase in articles over the next few months. Apple's marketing campaign took advantage of the spiritual associations. Its "Touching Is Believing" ad that year showed an index finger touching an illumined iPhone, an image that several bloggers likened to Michelangelo's *Creation of Adam*. And that would not be Apple's last religious reference. The company would turn to a different spiritual leader for its 1998 "Think Different" campaign, which put the Dalai Lama's smiling face on billboards around the world.

The Information Age also allowed new modes of performing rituals and gathering communities. By the 1990s there was religion online, which entailed accessing information about religion on the Internet—a Muslim visiting Toronto, for instance, could look up the local time for morning prayer. But there was also online religion, providing more interactive computer-mediated ritual. Online worshippers could light a virtual candle beneath the Virgin Mary's image and then leave a prayer request that other users could see, and Hindus could do *pūjā*, bringing offerings to a god by clicking on a piece of fruit and moving it to the altar of that digital deity. Even though the technology did not allow full multisensorial immersion, sites also promised "virtual pilgrimage" to an online sacred space, including an online *ḥajj* that helped the cyber-pilgrim to experience the sights and sounds of that multistep ritual. Millions also lived alternate lives on multi-user domains, or virtual worlds. In a nod to the spiritual, they even used a Sanskrit term that refers to the "descent of a deity" (*avatāra*) to describe their chosen online identities, and those "avatars" could even build a worship space, conduct a ritual, and attract a congregation.

The technological shift also introduced new modes of gathering. These spiritual communities were as diverse as the interactive technologies that generated them. Mobile phone texting, social media posting, and electronic mail allowed individuals and groups to connect, and telepresence software mediated midweek committee collaborations as well as weekend worship services. With the evolution of robotics after 2007, even more varied forms of interaction were emerging. "Always-on" mobile devices and home robots were becoming a first source of religious information, and the more sophisticated "social robots" being created on university campuses and at corporate headquarters were changing human-machine interactions even more. Along with robot therapists for the elderly suffering from dementia, Buddhists and Christians introduced robotic spiritual leaders like Mindar, who gives dharma talks at Kōdaiji, a four-hundred-year-old Zen temple in Kyoto, and BlessU-2, a robotic priest that gives blessings in five languages. Event organizers unveiled this mechanized-pastor in Wittenberg, Germany, on the five-hundred-year-anniversary of Martin Luther's initiating of the Protestant Reformation, a global spiritual movement that achieved its success because of the printing press, an earlier revolution in communication technology.

Integration and fragmentation in the Information Age

The new era we are living in has been called the Information Age or the Digital Age—labels that emphasize computation and communication technologies, which makes sense, since this technological shift has altered everyday life. The changes have been both exhilarating and worrisome and include not only creative new modes of religious expression and a heightened sense of connectivity, even among users in the developing world, but also, as research shows, an increased sense of isolation and a reduced capacity for intimacy among "digital natives," or those who have grown up with the new technology.

However, the shift to digital technology is not the only development now affecting our world. The rise of the service economy, including an underregulated global finance industry, has contributed to the mounting disparity between haves and have-nots. Advances in medicine, including gene editing, present troubling questions about the ethics of genetic modifications. International organizations that deliver humanitarian aid to the displaced have called this the "age of the migrant," and contributors to global affairs journals have warned about the erosion of democracy, the reemergence of autocracy, and new forms of ethno-religious nationalism. Scientists and UN officials warn that this generation is being defined by its response to environmental issues, including the ways that ecological degradation and climate change are disproportionately affecting women, children, and the poor.

And many observers, of course, decry the continuing outbreak of holy wars and point to religion as a primary source of contemporary divisions.

They have a point. There seems to be more conflict than connection. When political scientists who study religion search for ways to describe this post–Cold War era, few emphasize the power of digitally mediated communications to bring people together; instead, most highlight religion-based conflict. In fact, the most widely discussed interpretation from the mid-1990s to the post-9/11 era described a new world order defined not by differences between states but by the "clash of civilizations," as the political scientist Samuel P. Huntington put it. He argued that "cultural identities, which at their broadest level are civilizational identities, are shaping the patterns of cohesion, disintegration, and conflict," and he noted that most of the eight main civilizational identities are shaped by religion—including the two that are clashing most forcefully, Islamic Civilization and the Christian "West." This influential mapping of the fault lines drew as many critics as supporters, in part because of the author's call for a "renewal of Western identity."

More recent attempts to understand the "disintegrating" effects of religiously "cohesive" cultures have relied on global survey data to show that competing values have formed three distinctive "cultures" that cross the usual religious lines. This interpretation, published two decades after the "clash of civilizations" theory, suggests that the survey evidence points to three main global cultures, which disagree about the importance of tradition, the significance of material success, and the role of human interaction. Its author, Miguel E. Basáñez, explains the contemporary fragmentation in terms of the varying "cultures of honor" (Hinduism, Eastern Orthodoxy, and Islam), which cherish tradition and hierarchy and uphold preindustrial values; the "cultures of achievement" (Protestantism, Confucianism, and Judaism), which care about hard work and delayed gratification and cherish industrial values; and the postindustrial "cultures of joy" (Buddhism and Catholicism), which value family and social interaction. If we added socialist "cultures of parity," which value "classlessness" and display some but not all features of religion, we might have an even broader picture. Yet while such attempts at classification provoke conversation, and remind us to remain open to unexpected parallels—between Muslims and Hindus, for example—the three-cultures hypothesis, like the clashing civilization argument, minimizes diversity within as well as across traditions and oversimplifies religion's role in the transitions from farming to factories to fiber optics.

But these interpreters are right to note diverging values and disturbing divisions—which are hard to miss. There is evidence that fragmenting forces, some of them religious, are pulling us apart. Yet, as many interpreters fail to mention, it is more complicated than that. There are integrating forces at work too, and religion plays a disproportionate role in those efforts to bring us together.

Sadly, both digital connectivity and ethno-religious cohesion have been among the forces for fragmentation. Computer technologies, which were inspired by a spiritual vision that was supposed to bring us together, have not only prompted a loss of intimacy but also a loss of privacy, and that has implications for political life. While social media have been used to promote the common good—to protest human rights and organize democratic resistance, for example—some nations, nonstate actors, and transnational corporations are making surveillance more common and dissent more dangerous. Digital technologies have been weaponized. They have been used to shift popular opinion, influence democratic elections, silence free speech, discourage migrant movements, and inhibit religious worship. With the rise in ethno-religious nationalism, which has triggered both populist and autocratic impulses, religious freedom and ethnic tolerance are also being threatened. Recent research has quantified the increasing "government restrictions" on religion as well the harder-to-capture "social hostilities" involving religion. The most restrictive governments, according to an important study, include China, Iran, and Russia, and the nations that score highest on the "social hostilities" index include India and Pakistan as well as Israel and Egypt. But the survey results might not prompt celebration in all countries that cherish their reputation as more legally inclusive or socially tolerant: the United States and United Kingdom both rank as "moderately" restrictive and "high" on the social hostilities index. Overall, the evidence suggests that hostility toward people of different ethnic or religious backgrounds is surging around the world. In some ways, we seem further apart than ever.

Yet, as some analysts fail to note, religious actors also are challenging the forces of fragmentation. In other words, some religious groups have been not just cohesive, forming in-group bonds with the spiritually like-minded, but also adhesive, forming bonds with those of other faiths to work on shared global problems. Religious organizations and interfaith alliances have partnered with government leaders, intergovernmental agencies, and philanthropic foundations to address a range of continuing and emerging problems. Religious NGOs and intergovernmental agencies have collaborated to help displaced refugees, for example, and spiritually inspired public health initiatives have used community-based care to support those suffering from infectious diseases.

The religious also have mobilized to slow environmental degradation, even if some governments and many adherents refuse to abandon their faith in fossil fuels. In the same year that the UN's member states approved the seventeen "Sustainable Development Goals" they aspired to meet by 2030, including "climate action" and "reduced inequality," Pope Francis's encyclical *Laudato Si': On Care for Our Common Home* articulated an "integral ecology" that called for environmental restoration and social justice. In a welcome change, religious actors have been brought into global conversations about environmental repair, disaster relief, and poverty alleviation, and are playing a somewhat larger role in discussions about development and peacebuilding. Promising approaches to peacebuilding emphasize "restorative practices" that aim for reconciliation by acknowledging past wrongs, and new tools for interreligious dialogue have emerged. The advocates of "scriptural reasoning" invite diverse adherents to read sacred texts together as a way of "learning to disagree better." And individuals and small groups have reached across religious boundaries, as seen in Israeli-Arab peace organizations that are working to reverse entrenched patterns. Palestinian-born Muslims are forming closer ties with Israelis, for example, and Israeli-born Jews are arguing for "solidarity with Palestinians." Despite reasonable worries about the loss of intimacy and privacy, digital innovations such as translation apps and meeting software also have begun to transform social interaction around the world, sometimes in ways that the utopian-minded promoters originally had hoped.

So, at the onset of this Information Age, when we face unresolved crises inherited from the colonial and industrial eras—and are bequeathing new problems to those who follow us—there are still reasons for hope. Adherents around the world are mobilizing religion's resources to meet the challenges in this era, when we are brought together by fiber optic cables, global consumer culture, and interfaith peace efforts, but also pulled apart by rising nationalisms, climate change, and holy wars. It remains to be seen, of course, whether the forces for adhesion—those advocates of sticky religion—will be able to create new bonds that close the gaps and heal the wounds.

References

Preface

Samuel Purchas, *Purchas his pilgrimage, or, Relations of the world and the religions observed in all ages and places discovered, from the creation unto this present* (London: William Stansby, 1613).

Chapter 1

Jacob K. Olupona, *African Religions: A Very Short Introduction* (New York: Oxford University Press, 2014).

Zora Neale Hurston, *The Sanctified Church: The Folklore Writings of Zora Neale Hurston* (Berkeley, CA: Turtle Island, 1981), 15–17.

Anna Sun, *Confucianism as a World Religion: Contested Histories and Contemporary Realities* (Princeton, NJ: Princeton University Press, 2013).

James H. Leuba, *A Psychological Study of Religion: Its Origin, Function, and Future* (New York: AMS Press, 1969), 339–63.

Daniel Dubuisson, *The Western Construction of Religion: Myths, Knowledge, and Ideology*, trans. William Sayers (Baltimore: Johns Hopkins University Press, 2003), 17–18.

Sigmund Freud, *The Future of an Illusion* (New York: W. W. Norton, 1989), 42, 55, 56, 62.

Karl Marx and Friedrich Engels, *On Religion* (New York: Schocken, 1964), 42.

Émile Durkheim, *The Elementary Forms of Religious Life* (New York: Free Press, 1995), 44.

Clifford Geertz, *The Interpretation of Cultures* (New York: Basic Books, 1973), 90.

Martin Riesebrodt, *The Promise of Salvation: A Theory of Religion* (Chicago: University of Chicago Press, 2010), 72, 74–75.

Christian Smith, *Religion: What It Is, How It Works, and Why It Matters* (Princeton, NJ: Princeton University Press, 2017), 22.

Danièle Hervieu-Léger, *Religion as a Chain of Memory* (New Brunswick, NJ: Rutgers University Press, 2000), 82.

F. Max Müller, *Lectures on the Origin and Growth of Religion . . .* (New York: Charles Scribner's Sons, 1879), 1.

Rudolf Otto, *The Idea of the Holy* (Oxford: Oxford University Press, 1923), 5–7.

Mircea Eliade, *The Sacred and the Profane: The Nature of Religion* (New York: Harcourt, 1959), 10–13.

E. B. Tylor, *Primitive Culture* (London: John Murray, 1920), 1:424.

Pascal Boyer, *Religion Explained: The Evolutionary Origins of Religious Thought* (New York: Basic Books, 2001).

David Hume, *Dialogues and Natural History of Religion* (Oxford: Oxford University Press, 1993), 139.

Paul Tillich, *Theology of Culture* (New York: Oxford University Press, 1959), 7–8.

William James, *The Varieties of Religious Experience* (New York: Penguin, 1982), 31.

Melford E. Spiro, "Religion: Problems of Definition and Explanation," in *Anthropological Approaches to the Study of Religion*, ed. Michael Banton (London: Tavistock, 1966), 88, 96.

Thomas A. Tweed, *Crossing and Dwelling: A Theory of Religion* (Cambridge, MA: Harvard University Press, 2006), 54–79.

Randall Styers, *Making Magic: Religion, Magic, and Science in the Modern World* (New York: Oxford University Press, 2004).

Pew Research Center, "Being Christian in Western Europe," May 29, 2018, 119–38, https://www.pewforum.org/2018/05/29/attitudes-toward-spirituality-and-religion/.

Nancy Ammerman, "'Spiritual but Not Religious?': Beyond Binary Choices in the Study of Religion," *Journal for the Scientific Study of Religion* 52, no. 2 (2013): 258–78.

Chapter 2

Wendy Doniger, trans., *The Laws of Manu* (New York: Penguin, 1991), 3, 4, 6–7, 243.

Thomas A. Tweed, "Afterword: The Study of Religion and the Discourses of Indigeneity," in *Handbook of Indigenous Religions*, ed. Greg Johnson and Siv Ellen Kraft (Leiden, The Netherlands: Brill, 2017), 383–84 (religion and niche construction).

F. John Odling-Smee, Kevin N. Laland, and Marcus W. Feldman, *Niche Construction: The Neglected Process in Evolution* (Princeton, NJ: Princeton University Press, 2003).

Report of the World Commission on Environment and Development: Our Common Future, April 1987, p. 16 (paragraph 27), http://www.un-documents.net/our-common-future.pdf ("sustainability").

Geertz, *The Interpretation of Cultures*, 90.

Nestor Quiroa, "Missionary Exegesis of the Popol Vuh: Maya-K'iche' Cultural and Religious Continuity in Colonial and Contemporary Highland Guatemala," *History of Religions* 53, no. 1 (2013): 66–97.

Thomas Aquinas, *Summa Theologiæ*, Latin text and English translation (London: Blackfriars—Eyre and Spottiswoode, 1964), 3:90–93. (First Part, Question 13, Article 11: "He who is" and "an ocean of being").

Eihei Dōgen, *Shōbōgenzō*, Book 13, "Ocean Seal Samadhi," trans. Carl Bielefeldt with Michael Radich, *Soto Zen Journal* 14 (2004), https://global.sotozen-net.or.jp/eng/dharma/pdf/de14/de14_10.htm.

Aquinas, *Summa Theologiæ*, 2:90–93 (First Part, Question 6, Article 4: "likeness to God").

Matthew Arnold, *Selected Poems of Matthew Arnold* (London: Macmillan, 1898), 164–65 ("Dover Beach").

Elie Wiesel, *Night* (New York: Bantam, 1982), 32.

Mohandas K. Gandhi, *An Autobiography: The Story of My Experiments with Truth* (Boston: Beacon, 1957), 112.

Vinay Lal, "Gandhi's West, the West's Gandhi," *New Literary History* 40, no. 2 (2009): 281–313.

Henry David Thoreau, *"Walden," "Civil Disobedience," and Other Writings*, 3rd ed., ed. William Rossi (New York: Norton Critical Editions, 2008).

Leo Tolstoy, *The Kingdom of God Is within You* (New York: Charles Scribner's Sons, 1913), 19.

Laurie Patton, trans., *The Bhagavad Gita* (New York: Penguin, 2008).

Henry David Thoreau, *A Week on the Concord and Merrimack Rivers*, ed. Carl F. Hovde et al. (Princeton, NJ: Princeton University Press, 1980).

Laura Dassow Walls, *Henry David Thoreau: A Life* (Chicago: University of Chicago Press, 2017), 248–54.

Antoinette Burton, Faisal Devji, Mrinalini Sinha, Goolam Vahed, and Ashwin Desai, "Book Forum," Review of *The South African Gandhi: Stretcher-Bearer of Empire*, by Ashwin Desai and Goolam Vahed, *Journal of Natal and Zulu History* 32, no. 1 (2018): 105.

Melani McAlister, *The Kingdom of God Has No Borders: A Global History of American Evangelicals* (New York: Oxford University Press, 2018), 117–43 (on South Africa).

The Kairos Theologians, *Challenge to the Church: A Theological Comment on the Political Crisis in South Africa: The Kairos Document and Commentaries* (Geneva: World Council of Churches, 1985).

Chapter 3

E. Allison Peers, trans., "The Book of Her Life," in *The Complete Works of St. Teresa of Jesus* (London: Sheed and Ward, 1973), 1:192–93 (being "afire").

Tweed, *Crossing and Dwelling*, 93–103 (on spatial cognition and the body).

Jennifer M. Groh, *Making Space: How the Brain Knows Where Things Are* (Cambridge, MA: Harvard University Press, 2014), 189–201 (spatial cognition and memory).

Philip J. Ivanhoe and Bryan W. Van Norden, eds., *Readings in Classical Chinese Philosophy*, 2nd ed. (Indianapolis, IN: Hackett, 2005), 125 (Mengzi quotation).

Otto, *The Idea of the Holy*, 12–30 (quotation on page 12; the rest on *mysterium tremendum*).

Sigmund Freud, *Civilization and Its Discontents*, in *The Standard Edition of the Complete Psychological Works of Sigmund Freud*, ed. James Strachey (London: Hogarth Press, 1964), 21:64–68, 72–73 ("oceanic feeling").

Ayon Maharaj, "The Challenge of the Oceanic Feeling: Romain Rolland's Mystical Critique of Psychoanalysis and His Call for a 'New Science of the Mind,'" *History of European Ideas* 43, no. 5 (2017): 474–93 (on Freud and Rolland).

Ramakrishna, *The Sayings of Sri Ramakrishna* (Mylapore, India: Ramakrishna Math, 1916), 152.

Rūzbihān Baqlī, *The Unveiling of Secrets: Diary of a Sufi Master*, trans. Carl W. Ernst (Chapel Hill, NC: Parvardigar Press, 1997), 53 ("as a drop is to the ocean").

Nicolette D. Manglos-Weber, *Joining the Choir: Religious Membership and Social Trust among Transnational Ghanaians* (New York: Oxford University Press, 2018), 7, 22–27.

Kimberley Christine Patton and John Stratton Hawley, eds., *Holy Tears: Weeping in the Religious Imagination* (Princeton, NJ: Princeton University Press, 2005), 1–23, 25–51, 165–177.

E. Allison Peers, trans., *The Way of Perfection by Teresa of Avila* (1567; repr., New York: Image, 1964), 202 (tears at the presence of God).

Robert C. Fuller, *Wonder: From Emotion to Spirituality* (Chapel Hill: University of North Carolina Press, 2006), 38–41 ("association cortex" and wonder).

Durkheim, *Elementary Forms of Religious Life*, 218–28, 424 ("collective effervescence").

Sarvepalli Radhakrishnan, trans., *The Thirteen Principal Upaniṣads* (London: George Allen and Unwin, 1953), 623–25 (the charioteer restraining the senses, from the *Kaṭha Upaniṣad*).

Augustine of Hippo, *Confessions of Saint Augustine: Books I–X* (New York: Sheed and Ward, 1942), 135 ("chain" of habit).

Sally Promey, ed., *Sensational Religion: Sensory Cultures in Material Practice* (New Haven, CT: Yale University Press, 2014), 1–15 ("sensory cultures" of religion), 461–473 (ingesting relics and earth).

Don L. Smithers, "The Original Circumstances in the Performance of Bach's Leipzig Church Cantatas, 'Wegen Seiner Sonn—Und Festtägigen Amts-Verrichtungen,'" *Bach* 26, no. 1–2 (1995): 28–47.

John Blacking, *How Musical Is Man?* (London: Faber and Faber, 1976), 32, 42–43 ("ordered sound").

Susan Ashbrook Harvey, *Scenting Salvation: Ancient Christianity and the Olfactory Imagination* (Berkeley: University of California Press, 2006), 2–3 ("olfactory piety").

S. Brent Plate, *A History of Religion in 5/12 Objects: Bringing the Spiritual to Its Senses* (Boston: Beacon, 2014), 61–97 (incense).

Lian-Yu Lin et al., "Effects of Temple Particles on Inflammation and Endothelial Cell Response," *Science of the Total Environment* 414 (2012): 68–72 (effects of incense).

"Temples Selling Uncertified 'Eco-friendly' Incense," *Taipei Times*, January 16, 2016, 3.

Barbara G. Myerhoff, *Peyote Hunt: The Sacred Journey of the Huichol Indians* (Ithaca, NY: Cornell University Press, 1974), 112–264.

Hillary Kaell, *Walking Where Jesus Walked: American Christians and Holy Land Pilgrimage* (New York: New York University Press, 2014), 93–94 (pilgrims picking up stones and earth).

Nikky-Gurinder Kaur Singh, "Corporeal Metaphysics: Guru Nanak in Early Sikh Art," *History of Religions* 53, no. 1 (2013): 28–29 (aniconic quotation).

Diana L. Eck, *Banaras: City of Light* (Princeton, NJ: Princeton University Press, 1982), 20 (*darśan*).

John Reeve, *World Religions: British Museum Visitor's Guide* (London: British Museum Press, 2003).

Ninian Smart, *Dimensions of the Sacred: An Anatomy of the World's Beliefs* (Berkeley: University of California Press, 1996). My eight "modes of religious expression" revise and expand Smart's seven "dimensions of the sacred."

Terrance Deacon and Tyrone Cashman, "The Role of Symbolic Capacity in the Origin of Religion," *Journal for the Study of Religion, Nature, and Culture* 3 (2009): 1, 5, 26 (symbols and narratives).

Invild Sælid Gilhus, *Animals, Gods, and Humans: Changing Attitudes to Animals in Greek, Roman, and Early Christian Ideas* (London: Routledge, 2006), 172–75 (lamb of God).

Peter Harvey, *An Introduction to Buddhism: Teachings, History, and Practices* (Cambridge: Cambridge University Press, 1990), 47, 189–95 (Buddha as physician).

Elsaid M. Badawi and Muhammad Abdel Haleem, *Arabic-English Dictionary of Qurʾanic Usage* (Leiden, The Netherlands: Brill, 2008), 254–55 ("seal").

Carl W. Ernst, *Following Muhammad: Rethinking Islam in the Contemporary World* (Chapel Hill: University of North Carolina Press, 2003), 80–81 ("seal" and *sunna*), 108–62 (Islamic ethics).

Patton, *The Bhagavad Gita*.

Gloria Fraser Giffords, *Mexican Folk Retablos*, rev. ed. (Albuquerque: University of New Mexico Press, 1992), 143–47, 150 (on the *ex voto*).

J. G. Davies, "Architecture," in *Encyclopedia of Religion*, 2nd ed., ed. Lindsay Jones (New York: Macmillan 2004), 461, 466.

Religion

Julie Badiee and the editors, *"Mashriqu'l-Adhkár,"* Bahá'í
    Encyclopedia Project, http://www.bahai-encyclopedia-project.org.

Philip B. Yampolsky, trans., *The Platform Sutra of the Sixth Patriarch*
    (New York: Columbia University Press, 1967), 141–44.

Ivanhoe and Van Norden, *Readings in Classical Chinese Philosophy*,
    213, 219 (Zhuangzi quotations).

Harvey Whitehouse, *Modes of Religiosity: A Cognitive Theory of
    Religious Transmission* (Walnut Creek, CA: AltaMira Press,
    2004), 63–83 (low- and high-intensity rituals).

Max Weber, *Economy and Society: An Outline of Interpretive
    Sociology* (Berkeley: University of California Press, 1978), 1:54–56
    (political and religious organizations), 424–27 (priests), 439–51
    (prophets).

Llewelyn Morgan, *The Buddhas of Bamiyan* (Cambridge, MA:
    Harvard University Press, 2012), 72–73 ("forerunners" of
    Mahayana).

Mirwais Adeel, "Return of Bamiyan Buddhas with Help of 3D Image
    Display," Khamma Press News Agency, June 7, 2015, https://www
    .khaama.com/return-of-bamyan-buddhas-with-help-of-3d-image-
    display-9468/.

Chapter 4

Tweed, *Crossing and Dwelling*, 68 (on "figurative tools").

Agustín Fuentes, *The Creative Spark: How Imagination Made
    Humans Exceptional* (New York: Dutton, 2017), 25–48 (emer-
    gence and dispersal of human populations), 201–7 (earliest symbol
    use).

Henry de Lumley, "The Emergence of Symbolic Thought," in *Becoming
    Human: Innovation in Prehistoric Material and Spiritual Culture*,
    ed. Colin Renfrew and Iain Morley (Cambridge: Cambridge
    University Press, 2009), 17 ("metaphysical anguish").

Christopher Henshilwood et al., "Emergence of Modern Human
    Behavior: Middle Stone Age Engravings from South Africa,"
    Science 295 (2002): 1278–80 (Blombos Cave).

Vincent Formicola, "From the Sunghir Children to the Romito Dwarf:
    Aspects of the Upper Paleolithic Funerary Landscape," *Current
    Anthropology* 48, no. 3 (2007): 446–53 (Sunghir burial).

Walpurga Antl-Weiser, "The Time of the Willendorf Figurines and
    New Results of Paleolithic Research in Lower Austria,"
    Anthropologie 47, no. 1–2 (2009): 131–41 ("Venus of Willendorf").

Leore Grosman, Natalie D. Munro, and Anna Belfer-Cohen, "A 12,000-year-old Shaman Burial from the Southern Levant (Israel)," *Proceedings of the National Academy of Sciences* 105, no. 46 (2008): 17665–69 (the shaman burial).

Tom D. Dillehay and Dolores Piperno, "Agricultural Origins and Social Implications in South America," in *The Cambridge World Prehistory*, ed. Colin Renfrew and Paul Bahn (Cambridge: Cambridge University Press, 2014), 6:970–85 (global origins of agriculture).

Karl Schmidt, "Göbekli Tepe, Southeastern Turkey: A Preliminary Report on the 1995–1999 Excavations," *Paléorient* 26, no. 1 (2001): 45–54.

Ian Hodder, ed., *Religion at Work in a Neolithic Society: Vital Matters* (Cambridge: Cambridge University Press, 2014), 21, 58–83, 86–103, 134–52 (religion's role at Çatalhöyük and in Neolithic transition), 228–31 (mother and child burial).

Felipe Fernández-Armesto, *The World: A History* (Upper Saddle River, NJ: Prentice Hall, 2011), 46–75 (river valley civilizations).

Confucius (Kongzi), *The Analects*, trans. D. C. Lau (London: Penguin, 1979).

Philip J. Ivanhoe, trans., *The Daodejing of Laozi* (New York: Seven Bridges Press, 2002), xxii, 16 (*dao* as "root").

Ivanhoe and Van Norden, eds., *Readings in Classical Chinese Philosophy*, 112, 125, 143–45 (Mengzi on "sprouts" of virtue).

Charlotte Roberts and Keith Manchester, *The Archaeology of Disease*, 3rd ed. (Ithaca, NY: Cornell University Press, 2007), 16–17 ("less healthy" agriculturalists).

Bruce Lincoln, *Religion, Empire, and Torture: The Case of Archaemenian Persia, with a Postscript on Abu Ghraib* (Chicago: University of Chicago, 2007), xii–xv, 1–8 (quotations from inscriptions and analysis of Cyrus and Persian Empire).

N. A. Nikam and Richard McKeon, trans., *The Edicts of Asoka* (Chicago: University of Chicago Press, 1959), 27–30 (Rock Edict 13), 51–52 (Rock Edict 12).

María Rosa Menocal, *The Ornament of the World: How Muslims, Jews, and Christians Created a Culture of Tolerance in Medieval Spain* (New York: Back Bay Books, 2002), 32 ("ornament of the world").

Peter Jackson, trans., *The Mission of Friar William of Rubruck: His Journey to the Court of the Great Khan Möngke, 1253–1255* (Indianapolis, IN: Hackett, 2009).

Margot E. Fassler, *The Virgin of Chartres: Making History through Liturgy and the Arts* (New Haven, CT: Yale University Press, 2010), 152–55 (crusader song lyrics).

David Eltis and David Richardson, *Atlas of the Transatlantic Slave Trade* (New Haven, CT: Yale University Press, 2010), xvii (12.5 million Africans deported).

Mary B. Rose, *The Gregs of Quarry Bank Mill: The Rise and Decline of a Family Firm, 1750–1914* (Cambridge: Cambridge University Press, 1986), 16 (Greg's religion), 25 (the 1816 data), 113–16 (the chapels).

Uchida Hoshimi, "The Spread of Timepieces in the Meiji Period," *Japan Review* 14 (2002): 189–90 (sale of clocks and watches).

Nerilie Abram et al., "Early Onset of Industrial Era Warming across the Oceans and Continents," *Nature* 536 (August 25, 2016): 411–18 (global warming's onset).

Friedrich Engels, *The Condition of the Working Class in England* (1845; repr., Oxford: Oxford University Press, 2009), 245 ("absence" of religion).

C. A. Bayly, *The Birth of the Modern World, 1780–1914* (Malden, MA: Blackwell, 2004), 325 ("expansion" of religion).

"*Frank Leslie's Illustrated Newspaper* 1858 Cable News," History of the Atlantic Cable and Undersea Communications, https://atlantic-cable.com/Article/1858Leslies/index.htm (quotations about 1858 telegraph).

Jose C. Moya and Adam McKeown, *World Migration in the Long Twentieth Century: Essays on Global and Comparative History* (Washington, DC: American Historical Association, 2011), 1–15 (global migration statistics).

Andrew Ure, *The Philosophy of Manufactures: Or, an Exposition of the Scientific, Moral, and Commercial Economy of the Factory System of Great Britain* (London: C. Knight, 1835), 277 ("moral economy of the factory system"), 404–29 (religion in the factories).

Joseph Henrich, "Rice, Psychology, and Innovation," *Science* 344 (May 9, 2014): 593–94 (individualism, collectivism, and types of farming).

Nancy K. Stalker, *Japan: History and Culture from Classical to Cool* (Berkeley: University of California Press, 2018), 231 (quotation about thread and empire).

Henry A. Miles, *Lowell, As It Was, and As It Is*, 2nd ed. (Lowell, MA: Nathaniel L. Dayton, 1846), 142 ("moral machinery").

Kenneth Pomeranz, *The Great Divergence: China, Europe, and the Making of the Modern World Economy* (Princeton, NJ: Princeton University Press, 2000).

William Buckland, *Geology and Mineralogy Considered with Reference to Natural Theology* (London: William Pickering, 1836), 1:524–38 ("natural theology" of coal).

Thomas Parke Hughes, *Networks of Power: Electrification in Western Society, 1880–1930* (Baltimore, MD: Johns Hopkins University Press, 1983), 140–74 ("technological momentum").

Donald Worster, *Under Western Skies: Nature and History in the American West* (New York: Oxford University Press, 1992), 57–63 ("infrastructure trap").

David Livingstone, *The Last Journals of David Livingstone in Central Africa from 1865 to His Death* (London: J. Murray, 1874), 2:215 (Livingstone quotation).

Chinua Achebe, *The African Trilogy* (New York: Penguin, 2017), 155 ("all our gods are weeping").

Slobodan G. Markovich, "Coping with the Memory of Gavrilo Princip and the Symbolism of Vidovdan in Serbia and Yugoslavia," *South Slav Journal* 34, no. 1–2 (2015): 38, 41 (Gavrilo Princip, the assassin, as Serbian Orthodox "hero").

Chapter 5

Pew Research Center, "The Global Religious Landscape," 2012, http://www.globalreligiousfutures.org (For data and analysis from this earlier study, including some future projections).

Pew Research Center, "Pew-Templeton Global Religious Futures Project," 2016, http://www.globalreligiousfutures.org/ (For the statistics about religion, including the 2020 and 2050 projections).

United Nations, "The Universal Declaration of Human Rights," December 10, 1948, https://www.un.org/en/universal-declaration-human-rights/ ("inherent dignity").

"Is God Dead?," cover, *Time*, April 8, 1966.

Suren Rāghavan, *Buddhist Monks and the Politics of Lanka's Civil War: Ethnoreligious Nationalism of the Sinhala Sangha and Peacemaking in Sri Lanka, 1995–2010* (Sheffield, UK: Equinox, 2018), 63–70, 200–201 (the *Mahāvaṃsa*).

Vjekoslav Perica, "Religion in the Balkan Wars." *Oxford Handbooks Online*, October 2, 2014, https://www.oxfordhandbooks.com/

view/10.1093/oxfordhb/9780199935420.001.0001/
oxfordhb-9780199935420-e-37.

"Recalling 'Responsibility to Protect' UN Pays Tribute to Victims of
Srebrenica Genocide," UN News, July 1, 2015, https://news.un.org/
en/story/2015/07/503292-recalling-responsibility-protect-un-
pays-tribute-victims-srebrenica-genocide (The quotation from the
UN secretary-general).

Bruce Lawrence, ed., *Messages to the World: The Statements of Osama
Bin Laden* (London: Verso, 2005), xi–xxiii (Bin Laden), 3–14 (first
public message).

Monica Duffy Toft, Daniel Philpott, and Timothy Samuel Shah, *God's
Century: Resurgent Religion and Global Politics* (New York:
W. W. Norton, 2011), 147–73 (religious civil wars), 174–206
(religious efforts for peace and justice).

"Ten Inspiring Examples of Faiths Coming Together," Remembering
Srebrenica, 2019, https://www.srebrenica.org.uk/news/ten-
inspiring-examples-of-faiths-coming-together/ (Catholics,
Muslims, and Jews at Srebenica).

Sulak Sivaraksa, *A Buddhist Vision for Renewing Society: Collected
Articles by a Concerned Thai Intellectual* (Bangkok: Thai Inter-
Religious Commission for Development, 1994).

Andries Odendall, *An Architecture for Building Peace at the Local
Level: A Comparative Study of Local Peace Committees* (New York:
United Nations Development Programme, 2010), 40–43 (Wajir
Peace and Development Committee).

United Nations Intergovernmental Panel on Climate Change, https://
www.ipcc.ch.

Fredrik Albritton Jonsson, *The Enlightenment's Frontier: The Scottish
Highlands and the Origins of Environmentalism* (New Haven, CT:
Yale University Press, 2013), 121–29 (rival ecologies of Kalm and
Smith).

Martin Palmer with Victoria Finlay, *Faith in Conservation: New
Approaches to Religions and the Environment* (Washington, DC:
World Bank, 2003), 97–106 (Qurʾānic quotation and Islamic
statement).

Fred Turner, *From Counterculture to Cyberculture: Stewart Brand, the
Whole Earth Network, and the Rise of Digital Utopianism*
(Chicago: University of Chicago Press, 2006).

Erik Davis, *TechGnosis: Myth, Magic, and Mysticism in the Age of
Information* (Berkeley, CA: North Atlantic Books, 2015), xxi
("technomysticism").

Steve Jobs, "Commencement Address," Stanford University, June 12, 2005, https://news.stanford.edu/2005/06/14/jobs-061505/ (quotation about *Whole Earth Catalog*).

Whole Earth Catalog, "Purpose," (Fall 1968): 2 ("we are as gods").

Marc Andreesen, "Why Software Is Eating the World," *Wall Street Journal*, August 20, 2011, https://www.wsj.com/articles/SB100014 24053111903480904576512250915629460 ("six decades into the computer revolution . . .").

Judy Wajcman, "How Silicon Valley Sets Time," *New Media and Society* 21, no. 6 (2019): 1281 (calendars "like a whole religion almost").

John Bunyan, *The Pilgrim's Progress* (Oxford: Oxford University Press, 2003).

Liberty S. Savard, *God's GPS for Your Soul II* (Sacramento, CA: Liberty Savard Publishing, 2015).

Sant Rajinder Singh Ji, "Downloading God," *Daily Excelsior*, October 15, 2015, https://www.dailyexcelsior.com/downloading-god/.

Heidi A. Campbell and Antonio C. La Pastina, "How the iPhone Became Divine: New Media, Religion, and the Intertextual Circulation of Meaning," *New Media and Society* 12, no. 7 (2010): 1191–207 ("Jesus phone").

Thomas A. Tweed, "Buddhism, Art, and Transcultural Collage: Toward a Cultural History of Buddhism in the United States, 1945–2000," in *Gods in America: Religious Pluralism in the United States*," ed. Charles L. Cohen and Ronald L. Numbers (New York: Oxford University Press, 2013), 212 ("Think Different" and Dalai Lama).

Alastair Himmer, "Kyoto Temple Puts Faith in Robot Priest . . . ," *Japan Times*, August 15, 2019, https://www.japantimes.co.jp/news/2019/08/15/business/tech/kyoto-temple-puts-faith-robot-priest-drawing-praise-japanese-scorn-westerners/#.XWw91S2ZNBw.

Harriet Sherwood, "Robot Priest Unveiled in Germany to Mark 500 Years since Reformation," *The Guardian*, May 30, 2017, https://www.theguardian.com/technology/2017/may/30/robot-priest-blessu-2-germany-reformation-exhibition.

Pew Research Center, "In Emerging Economies, Smartphone and Social Media Users Have Broader Social Networks," August 2019, https://www.pewinternet.org/2019/08/22/in-emerging-economies-smartphone-and-social-media-users-have-broader-social-networks/.

Shirley Turkle, *Alone Together: Why We Expect More from Technology and Less from Each Other*, 3rd ed. (New York: Basic Books, 2017), xx–xxvi (loss of intimacy and privacy).

Samuel P. Huntington, *The Clash of Civilizations and the Remaking of World Order* (New York: Simon & Schuster, 1996).

Miguel E. Basáñez, *A World of Three Cultures: Honor, Achievement, and Joy* (New York: Oxford University Press, 2016).

Pew Research Center, "A Closer Look at How Religious Restrictions Have Risen around the World," July 15, 2019, 85–87 (Government Restrictions Index), 88–90 (Social Hostilities Index), https://www.pewforum.org/2019/07/15/a-closer-look-at-how-religious-restrictions-have-risen-around-the-world/.

United Nations, "Sustainable Development Goals," 2015, https://sustainabledevelopment.un.org/?menu=1300.

Pope Francis, *Laudato Si': On Care for Our Common Home*, encyclical letter, May 24, 2015 (Huntington, IN: Our Sunday Visitor, 2015), 93–108 ("integral ecology").

"Scriptural Reasoning," http://www.scripturalreasoning.org ("disagreeing better").

Atalia Omer, *Days of Awe: Reimagining Jewishness in Solidarity with Palestinians* (Chicago: University of Chicago Press, 2019), 7, 39–67 ("solidarity for Palestinians").

Further reading

Preface

Amore, Roy C., Amir Hussain, and Williard G. Oxtoby, eds. *A Concise Introduction to World Religions*, 4th ed. New York: Oxford University Press, 2019.

Dinham, Adam, and Matthew Francis, eds. *Religious Literacy in Policy and Practice*. Bristol, UK: Policy Press, 2016.

Jones, Lindsay, ed. *The Encyclopedia of Religion*, 2nd ed. 15 vols. Detroit: Macmillan Reference, 2005.

Sharpe, Eric J. *Comparative Religion: A History*, 2nd ed. La Salle, IL: Open Court Press, 1986.

Smith, Jonathan Z. ed., *The HarperCollins Dictionary of Religion*. San Francisco: HarperSanFrancisco, 1995.

Ward, Graham. *Theology and Religion: Why It Matters*. Cambridge: Polity Press, 2019.

Chapter 1

Jantzen, Grace M. *Becoming Divine: Towards a Feminist Philosophy of Religion*. Bloomington: Indiana University Press, 1999.

Lambek, Michael, ed. *A Reader in the Anthropology of Religion*. Malden, MA: Blackwell, 2008.

Olupona, Jacob K., and Terry Rey, eds. *Òrìṣà Devotion as World Religion: The Globalization of Yorùbá Religious Culture*. Madison: University of Wisconsin Press, 2008.

Pals, Daniel. *Nine Theories of Religion*, 3rd ed. New York: Oxford University Press, 2015.

Stausberg, Michael, and Steven Engler, eds. *The Oxford Handbook of the Study of Religion*. Oxford: Oxford University Press, 2016.

Tweed, Thomas A. *Crossing and Dwelling: A Theory of Religion*. Cambridge, MA: Harvard University Press, 2006.

Chapter 2

Asad, Talal. *Genealogies of Religion: Discipline and Reasons of Power in Christianity and Islam*. Baltimore: Johns Hopkins University Press, 1993.

Chidester, David. *Savage Systems: Colonialism and Comparative Religion in Southern Africa*. Charlottesville, VA: University of Virginia Press, 1996.

Harvey, Paul, and Kathryn Gin Lum. *The Oxford Handbook of Religion and Race in American History*. New York: Oxford University Press, 2018.

Heine, Steven, ed. *Dōgen: Textual and Historical Studies*. New York: Oxford University Press, 2012.

King, Richard. *Orientalism and Religion: Postcolonial Theory, India, and "The Mystic East."* London: Routledge, 1999.

McGinn, Bernard. *Thomas Aquinas's "Summa theologiae": A Biography*. Princeton, NJ: Princeton University Press, 2014.

Orsi, Robert A. *Between Heaven and Earth: The Religious Worlds People Make and the Scholars Who Study Them*. Princeton, NJ: Princeton University Press, 2007.

Weber, Timothy. *Gandhi as Disciple and Mentor*. Cambridge, UK: Cambridge University Press, 2004.

Chapter 3

Beck, Gary, ed. *Sacred Sound: Experiencing Music in World Religions*. Waterloo, ON: Wilfrid Laurier University Press, 2006.

Corrigan, John, ed. *The Oxford Handbook of Religion and Emotion*. Oxford: Oxford University Press, 2008.

Freiberger, Oliver, ed. *Asceticism and Its Critics: Historical Accounts and Comparative Perspectives*. New York: Oxford University Press, 2006.

Jamison, Stephanie W., and Joel P. Brereton. *The Rigveda: the Earliest Religious Poetry of India*. New York: Oxford University Press, 2014.

McGinn, Bernard. *The Presence of God: A History of Western Christian Mysticism*. 7 vols. New York: Herder and Herder, 2004–2016.

McHugh, James. *Sandalwood and Carrion: Smell in Indian Religion and Culture*. New York: Oxford University Press, 2012.

Morgan, David. *The Sacred Gaze: Religious Visual Culture in Theory and Practice*. Berkeley: University of California Press, 2005.

Plate, S. Brent, ed. *Key Terms in Material Religion*. London: Bloomsbury, 2015.

Rappaport, Roy A. *Ritual and Religion in the Making of Humanity*. Cambridge: Cambridge University Press, 1999.

Taves, Ann. *Religious Experience Reconsidered: A Building-Block Approach to the Study of Religion and Other Special Things*. Princeton, NJ: Princeton University Press, 2009.

Chapter 4

Alcock, Susan E., et al. *Empires: Perspectives from Archaeology and History*. Cambridge: Cambridge University Press, 2001.

Beckert, Sven. *Empire of Cotton: A Global History*. New York: Vintage, 2014.

Carrasco, Davíd. *Religions of Mesoamerica*, 2nd ed. Long Grove, IL: Waveland Press, 2014.

Freeman, Joshua B. *Behemoth: A History of the Factory and the Making of the Modern World*. New York: W. W. Norton, 2018.

Fuentes, Agustín. *Why We Believe: Evolution and the Human Way of Being*. New Haven, CT: Yale University Press, 2019.

Hodder, Ian. *Religion in the Emergence of Civilization: Çatalhöyük as a Case Study*. Cambridge: Cambridge University Press, 2010.

Insoll, Timothy, ed. *The Oxford Handbook of the Archaeology of Ritual and Religion*. Oxford: Oxford University Press, 2011.

Norenzayan, Ara. *Big Gods: How Religion Transformed Cooperation and Conflict*. Princeton, NJ: Princeton University Press, 2013.

Rosenberg, Emily S. *A World Connecting, 1870–1945*. Cambridge, MA: Harvard University Press, 2012.

Thapar, Romila. *Aśoka and the Decline of the Mauryas*, 3rd ed. New Delhi: Oxford University Press, 2015.

Chapter 5

Berger, Peter, Grace Davie, and Effie Fokas. *Religious America, Secular Europe?: A Theme and Variations*. Aldershot, UK: Ashgate, 2008.

Griffin, Michael, and Jennie Weiss Block, eds. *In the Company of the Poor: Conversations with Dr. Paul Farmer and Fr. Gustavo Gutiérrez.* Maryknoll, NY: Orbis, 2013.

Hart, John, ed. *The Wiley Blackwell Companion to Religion and Ecology.* Hoboken, NJ: John Wiley and Sons, 2017.

Jian, Chen, et al., eds. *The Routledge Handbook of the Global Sixties: Between Protest and Nation-Building.* New York: Routledge, 2018.

Johnson, Greg, and Siv Ellen Kraft, eds. *Handbook of Indigenous Religions.* Leiden, The Netherlands: Brill, 2017.

Kivisto, Peter. *Religion and Immigration: Migrant Faiths in North America and Western Europe.* Malden, MA: Polity Press, 2014.

Kong, Lily. *Religion and Space: Competition, Conflict, and Violence in the Contemporary World.* London: Bloomsbury, 2016.

Mahmood, Saba. *Politics of Piety: The Islamic Revival and the Feminist Subject.* Princeton, NJ: Princeton University Press, 2011.

Omer, Atalia, R. Scott Appleby, and David Little, eds., *Oxford Handbook of Religion, Conflict, and Peacebuilding.* New York: Oxford University Press, 2015.

Pew-Templeton Global Religious Futures Project, "The Future of World Religions," available at http://www.globalreligiousfutures.org.

Woodhead, Linda, Christopher H. Partridge, and Hiroko Kawanami, eds. *Religions in the Modern World: Traditions and Transformations*, 3rd ed. New York: Routledge, 2016.

Index

Religion

Index

Index

W

Wahhabism, 99
Walden (Thoreau), 26
war, 96–100. *See also* violence
   examples of, 28, 81, 97, 98,
     99, 100
   religion and, xxi, 21, 28, 48, 76,
     78, 79, 81, 100
   and World Wars, 25, 81,
     89, 90, 100
Weber, Max, 60
white supremacy, 29–30.
    See also race
Whole Earth Catalog, 102

Wiesel, Elie, 25
William of Rubruck, 78
women, 11, 17, 50, 60, 69, 87, 95,
   101, 107. *See also* gender
worship spaces, 3, 12, 51, 60, 62,
   86, 105. *See also* architecture
World Wide Web, 103

Z

Zen (Chan), 23–24, 53–54, 61–62,
   102, 105
Zhuangzi, 53–54
Zoroastrianism, 17, 50, 51, 61,
   76, 91

Religion